Twelve Steps to Inner Peace

With Empowering Spiritual Tools

Premlatha Rajkumar

and

Sheryl Lynn Christian

Copyright © 2012 P. Rajkumar, S.L. Christian
All rights reserved.
No part of this book may be used or reproduced in any manner whatsoever without written permission. No part of this book may be stored in a retrieval system or transmitted in any form or by any means including electronic, electrostatic, magnetic tape, mechanical, photocopying, recording, or otherwise without the prior permission in writing of the publisher.

Edited by Sheryl Lynn Christian
Published by C.A. Books, San Diego, CA
For information address:
C.A. Books
3525 Del Mar Heights Rd. Suite 407
San Diego, California 92130
slchristian@cabooks.pub
http://www.christianashleybooks.com

Black and White, 2nd Ed. 12.12.12
ISBN-13: 978-1481148085
ISBN-10: 1481148087

DEDICATION

Heroes of the ancient world wore masks, costumes, heavy armors, and were licensed to kill. True Heroes of the New World are those who strive to shine the light of truth and wisdom. They are those who constantly pray for peace and harmony for their human family, and they are those who are not afraid to reach out with compassion and love toward an enemy. For they know that darkness can be won only by illuminating themselves and thereby reflecting the world with their light.
~Premlatha Rajkumar

Our gratitude goes to all of the True Heroes of the World for their unconditional love and service to the Planet.
With immense gratitude from our hearts we acknowledge
Benevolent beings who channel love and wisdom for the planet ~
Seth, Abraham, Bashar, and Kryon;
The channeled material of *A Course In Miracles*;
Great Teachers of centuries past ~
Carl Jung, Joseph Campbell, Rudolf Steiner, Khalil Gibran, Rumi, and Mahatma Gandhi;
Our gratitude to the priceless contributions of Teachers who share their unconditional love and light for the awakening of humanity ~
Eckhart Tolle, His Holiness the Dalai Lama, Osho, Louise Hay, Jim Self, Gregg Braden, Drunvalo Melchizedek, John Lennon, Shakti Gawain, Marianne Williamson, Dr. Mitchell Gibson, Byron Katie, Neale Donald Walsch, Dr. Joseph Murphy, Zakairan, Andrew Flaxman, Catherine Sainberg, Thich Nhat Hanh, Nikitha S. Prema, Dr. Deepak Chopra, Leonard Jacobson, Master Mooji, Elizabeth Clare Prophet, and Dolores Cannon.

Our love and gratitude also goes to our loving families for their love and support as they are the heroes whose presence blesses us each day.

Writing this book has been a grand journey of responsibility, awareness, and personal empowerment. We present this book as a work of love that offers probable solutions for transforming and empowering your life.

The information contained in this book has been provided for educational purpose only. It is not intended to treat, diagnose, cure or prevent any disease.

CONTENTS

	Introduction	vi
1	Forgiving	1
2	Belief and Trust	12
3	Allowing and Surrender	36
4	Gratitude	50
5	Deservedness	59
6	Loving the Self	72
7	Compassion	90
8	Awareness	108
9	Meditation and Silence	122
10	Conscious Connection	136
11	Relationships	162
12	Celebration	197
	Acknowledgements	215
	About the Authors	216

∞

A message from a benevolent entity

~Self Love Practice~

Self Love is accepting all of yourself and any part of yourself that you do not love. In so doing, you will heal that which you do not like within yourself. This will bring you peace.

The practice for self-love is simple. In front of a mirror, you are to say, "I love you," to your reflection. Do this for as many times and for as long as you need to.

Warmth shall envelop your heart with this practice. When you feel the warmth, you can rest until the next day. Do this practice once per day for as many days as you feel you need to.

Once you have developed a feeling of wholeness where love is complete within you, you are ready to fully experience life. Your sharing comes now from a place of love rather than need. ~Seth~ via Sheryl Christian

INTRODUCTION

This book is a powerful guide that provides a variety of spiritual tools to address your spiritual needs.

The spiritual tools provided here are proven overtime to change the quality of life. We invite you on this magical journey to discover how to put these tools to work and create the life of your dreams.

As a species we are a powerful group of entities. We are born with Divinity so powerful that we co-create the Planet with the Creator. Our power lies in our agreements. The world and the situations in the world exist because of our agreements. Our agreements can either be conscious or unconscious. Most of the time, our agreements are unconscious. We lost the art of living consciously due to programmed learning from the time we were born. Whether it was our parents, teachers, or religious leaders, the society around us drummed two things into us all of the time. These two things were that *we are not good enough* and that *we do not deserve.* This kind of programming has been going on for eons resulting in the chaos and confusion that we have created as a collective on this Planet. We were programmed to deny our joy and our divine nature. By denying our joy, we created situations that separated us from our Divinity.

Our sacred birthright is Inner Peace. In the words of the Mahatma Gandhi:

"An eye for an eye only makes the whole world blind!"

For hundreds of years, mankind has been playing this game of an eye for an eye, and has lost its power of sight. When we truly see our creation right now, it is mostly war, chaos, and confusion between individuals, families, clans, and nations. The only thing that can change the world on the outside is to change it on the inside of each one of us. It is a total transformation of consciousness for a new humanity working from the place of Inner Peace to create "Heaven on Earth".

Yes, we are absolutely the builders of "Heaven" on this Planet. Until we realize this, we will continue to be the losers. Life is not made on the platform of competition or comparison. If we continue to play the games of competition, comparison, scarcity, and war, then we all are going to be the losers.

When many of us choose to anchor peace in our inner being, we will create a more blissful existence. In the words of Osho:

> "People become suicidal for the simple reason that life is ugly, they do not know how to beautify it, how to make a song out of it. It is just sadness, a long-long anguish, a nightmare. People become interested in war and support war for any excuse; they are ready to kill and be killed."

No revolution on the outside can change our existence. Only the conscious choice to revolutionize on the inside and to create a peaceful space within us will enhance existence on the outside to blossom with beauty and joy.

We are the power in our life. Power does not mean to take control in order to feel secure. There is no security outside of us. We are the power and we create security. Our Creator created us in love and gave us the power to manifest whatever we want. This is our birthright; we are the creators of our reality. When we do not know this, we live in a world of illusion and feel that we are victims of situations and that things are being done to us. It is time to awaken. To know and to understand deep within that we manifest our reality. We came to this planet to live a wonderful life, and this wonderment and joy is within us. It can never come from the outside. Things on the outside are created from the inside. Therefore, as this is so, let us stop searching on the outside and start creating wonderment and joy from inside us.

When we search for that something that will bring harmony for our world on the outside, guidance leads us on a Spiritual Journey to come to peace with ourselves. To bring peace within, we work our way through these Twelve Steps. Forgiving, living in trust, surrendering to life, living the attitude of gratitude, acknowledging that we are absolutely worthy and deserving to receive the Grace and Favor of the Divine, loving the Self, being compassionate, becoming aware, living from the place of silence, conscious connection with the Planet and all beings, building the right relationship with ourselves and each other, and celebrating the beauty and wonderment of life are the steps. Let us meditate on these Twelve Steps and allow Peace to Happen.

These twelve chapters are designed to create inner balance and peace, and connection between people. ~Seth

From our experience with our spiritual journey, we understood that these twelve steps are wholesome and essential to wake up to our magnificence and empower ourselves as beautiful beings of love, joy, peace, and harmony. And it is our grandest intention that we share our experience with our beloved human family at this time.

We embrace each and every one of you into the love and light of our hearts.
Blessings! Namaste! In Love, Gratitude, and Peace,
Premlatha Rajkumar and Sheryl Christian

∞

1 FORGIVING

"As I walked out the door toward the gate that would lead to my freedom, I knew if I didn't leave my bitterness and hatred behind, I'd still be in prison." ~Nelson Mandela

"A life lived without forgiveness is a prison." ~William Arthur Ward

You forgive the person or situation not because what the person did was right, but you forgive to save yourself the suffering, heartache, and feelings of revenge. The pain that you focus on will never give you peace of mind and the more you bind your emotions to the pain, the more of it you will create in your life. So being angry and revengeful does not affect the person you are angry with. Instead, it destroys your life. Thus, you forgive to keep yourself in well being. Carrying hatred and anger is like carrying garbage wherever you go, it will stink your life. ~Premlatha Rajkumar

Forgiving others and ourselves is the first step toward the journey of Inner Peace.

WHY FORGIVE? THIS IS THE POWERFUL QUESTION OF THE MIND

"It is through the strength of God in me, which I am remembering as I forgive." ~ Lesson 60 ~*A Course In Miracles*

We live in the world but we, each and every one of us, create our own world inside our minds. The world outside is totally different from the world we create on the inside. The world outside is perfect, and everyone is being who they are exactly as they are supposed to be; there are no mistakes here, and we are all okay. But suffering comes when we choose to believe our judgments about the world outside and hold these as beliefs in our inner created world.

Our inner world is created by the mind that can only know a person or a situation through just the five physical senses. The data stored by the mind does not include the thoughts, emotions, or feelings of that person. So the data stored and believed by the mind is definitely insufficient. Taking this insufficient data as the truth, we make ourselves suffer and in doing so, we think that the world is the cause of our suffering. But the truth is, what we choose to believe about the world is the cause of our suffering – absolutely.

If we courageously and truthfully start inquiry into the belief data of our mind, we come to understand that not even one belief is completely true about ourselves or about anyone outside us. When we understand this, the world then becomes a kinder place. We come to understand that we were at war with the ways of the world, and we believed that the world was a crazy place. Yet the truth becomes clear that the world was not crazy; we became crazy by holding on to our beliefs about the world.

When we are not at war with the world outside, our inner world is peaceful, and it projects a peaceful outer world.

When there is inner peace, we come into the freedom of living in Grace and Ease; for we understand that what we have right now is what we wanted. Life is benevolent, and it always brings to us that which we need at the right time, nothing more, and nothing less.

So let us contemplate ~ are we willing to lose our mind-created world?

∞

KARMA AND RECOGNIZING THE GAME OF DUALITY

In India, people spoke a lot about karma. Karma refers to one's actions or deeds that trigger an entire cycle of cause and effect. It was said that karma was the reason that we are bound to the earth and that we take many life times to balance and get out of the cycle of cause and effect. It would more accurate to say that when we re-align with our Divine Presence we clear our karma.

The deeper truth is that *We are the Creators of Karma* through our severe judgments and condemning. For example, let us see the situation of a mother who gives her child up for adoption because she is unable to care for the baby. If she blesses the child to be well, and she is content with her decision and happy about what she did, then she has not created any karma. In contrast, if this mother is feeling guilty about her decision, and she is sorry for her child and feels a lifetime of remorse about giving her child up, then she has bound herself with "karma" to be balanced with another lifetime for her and the child.

Knowingly or unknowingly, we bind ourselves with so many harsh judgments and condemnations. This human tendency of constant judgment is the one that imprisons us to every kind of discord. If we point a finger at someone, immediately, three fingers of our own hand points back to us. Reality constantly reminds us to analyze our fear thoughts and center ourselves in peace. If we do not condemn, there will be no need to forgive.

In the words of Byron Katie:

> "Reality – the way that it is, exactly as it is, in every moment – is always kind. It's our story about reality that blurs our vision, obscures what's true, and leads us to believe that there is injustice in the world. When you believe that any suffering is legitimate, you become the champion of suffering, the perpetuator of it in yourself."

Karma is not a Universal Law. We choose to believe in it, and we have made it a belief system to build the game of Duality. By judging and condemning, we choose to punish and suffer. It takes awareness and immense trust in the Divine to accept life situations; to see the gift that every situation brings. We volunteered to be here in this body – in this lifetime now. We are not wounded, and we are not learning lessons or undergoing punishments; we are actually EVOLVING – evolving into our grander selves.

We are in total freedom. For through our challenges, we are exploring different levels of consciousness. Our challenges force us to question our mind and make us focus on the physical and the Spiritual. We are here to gather knowledge – to resolve our experiences by knowing ourselves at a much more conscious level. When we choose to be kind and non-judgmental in dealing with every aspect of life, we create freedom, harmony, and peace within; all of which powerfully reflect on the outside.

The mind loves to play the game of duality by telling stories. Stories about people, places, and situations – never-ending stories. It must be noted that the stories are all about judgments and condemnation; therefore, creating a world of suffering.

Thoughts argue with reality thus creating war within oneself. When we start loving what is in front of us – our reality – the war is over. It is always stressful and difficult to compete with and compare our situations, or to belittle our actions by contemplating what we should or should not have done.

The mind brings in a lot of story-thoughts. The thoughts come and they go like the clouds on a clear sky. We are the sky on which the thought clouds pass. Yes, they pass away all of the time; however, it is always our choice to attach or not attach our emotions to them. It is always our choice to live in true freedom – the freedom to know that we are the sky that allows yet never needs to be involved. Freedom is giving the gift of KINDNESS to oneself; it means never allowing fear, anger, or sadness to cloud your life. It means to live life with total acceptance, flexibility, and without resistance. There is no success to be achieved, and there is no failure either; for whatever we are doing at this moment with total love and acceptance is Success.

∞

IMPORTANCE OF KNOWING OUR MIND-CREATED WORLD

Let us take a committed journey into our inner world and liberate ourselves from the bondage of both emotional and physical pain. Our unresolved issues in life have a direct correlation to the health of our bodies and our wellbeing.

The key to our healing is to straight away deal with our wounds, to process our fears, forgive from the heart, and stand in our Truth. Only a courageous person, who is passionately seeking freedom, can take this journey of moving through unresolved fears.

Our physical bodies are formed not from the food and nutrients we take in, but from our life experiences, our attitudes to life, our emotions, and our pain buried from past experiences. It is a human tendency to hide behind wounds and create walls so thick that we are unable to move ahead in life.

We are powerful energy beings; but it is sad to notice that we give away our energy for things that do not support us in any way. We give away our creative energy to judge people, situations, places, and things. We lock them into wounded memories and attitudes. We do not realize that our wounds cost us a great deal both physically and monetarily.

Our health is intimately connected with our emotions and attitudes. Our unprocessed fears and emotions are injurious to our health and well-being. Our stress pours into our bodies as acid. Our blood pH is alkaline, and so to process the acid, the body organs struggle every day. Our bodies create fat cells to engulf the excess acid in the body and store it away from the vital organs and delicate systems of the body. Our bodies start holding fat and go into disease and distress.

Locking ones focus into a negative past, focusing all ones attention and energy on it, feeding it by talking about it, and exaggerating it every day, seems to be a most powerful pastime of our society and culture today! People feel that if there is nothing to grumble about or be negative about, then there will be nothing else to talk about with each other. We love to keep the wounds of the past alive, and we habitually create stories about them. Our habits have become our culture, and our culture has taught us not to care for ourselves or to take responsibility for our happiness. Being sad and having a whole bunch of tragic stories seems more purposeful. That is why we are so addicted to soap operas and movies that are highly dramatic and emotional. We always relate easily to what we hold on the inside.

We are energy beings, and our bodies thrive on life force energy. Our life force energy depends on our every thought, our emotions, and our attitudes. If we choose to encourage negative thoughts and emotions, we are in for great trouble. For these are more toxic to the body than any toxic food or drink. The more judgmental we become, the more energy will become depleted from our system. Our body becomes tired and weak, we become irritated and short tempered all of the time, and we even stop doing the things that we were usually doing. This is very serious because we are heavily losing our life force energy. Carrying negative beliefs and judgments cost a lot of energy. Gossiping and deliberately saying derogatory comments to people drains enormous amounts of energy. How we create heaven or hell in our lives does not depend on any religious practice; it solely depends on how we treat ourselves and others.

Being human is challenging as every person goes through trauma in life. The bitter thing about personal challenges is that people sometimes take the power from their trauma or challenges, build up stories around it, and use it to try to control other people. They have a "poor me" party for themselves; a viable reason and excuse to not be good or feel good. Our culture, society, and religious traditions teach us to feel guilty. We are burdened by guilt, and guilt never allows us to heal our wounds. Therefore, guilt is a wasted and a wasting emotion. This is why the saying, "Hurt people are the ones who hurt others," is true. The ugly truth here is that we become so connected with our wounded past that we use it to manipulate others.

Every person, every place, and every situation has been created benevolently by life for our growth physically, spiritually, and emotionally. Every interaction with another human being and every experience with every life situation is a beautiful opportunity to expand, to amass, and to gather enormous knowledge and wisdom. All we can deal with from the mind is only what we see in front of us – our minds do not know the bigger picture. If we truly analyze from our heart, we can know that our past has brought us to where we are right now, and this wisdom gives us a clue of how to create our future from this platform. Life has always been benevolent; reality or God is always loving and good, and there is no argument. When we argue with reality, we suffer greatly.

The only key to avoid suffering of the body, mind, and soul, is through forgiveness toward oneself and others. Pain is not an enemy – it is a bringer of wisdom and knowledge, and it is a guardian who shows us the way to freedom. Paying attention to life, living every moment fully and completely, allowing and accepting our reality, making room for forgiveness, choosing to focus our energy on our strengths and our gifts, and living from the place of gratitude, are the most powerful ways of healing and liberating ourselves from the illusion of fear and pain. When we liberate ourselves, our life force energy becomes powerful enough to liberate everyone who comes into our space!

Making peace with humanity and Divinity is the MAGIC OF LIFE.

SPIRITUAL TOOLS

When we forgive, we give back the energies of other people that we have kept "on hold" in our space, and we also take back our energies from their space. We become our whole selves, and we now have the grace to create our reality from the place of our power. We are energy beings and it is true that others energetically feel what we feel.

The spiritual tools must be used from the place of feeling – from the heart. Feeling is the key. Any tool, is just a tool until we put our energies – our hearts – our feelings into it.

AFFIRMATION

Affirmations are words that empower. However, words are just words until we bind them with our feelings. Therefore, every affirmation we say needs to be bound with our feelings, has to be said aloud or silent, or must be written many times a day. This helps to erase the past that has been programmed by many years of conditioning, and energetically rewrites the future that we want for ourselves.

Forgiveness Affirmations:

I forgive anyone whom I think has harmed me in this life or any lifetime, anywhere ever, in my space.
I forgive all debts; I erase all karmas.
I choose the Light of Understanding to light my path Now.

To specifically forgive someone who is in your space right now, do the following as many times a day as you can by pouring your feelings into every word and making it true for you. Do it; it works like magic.

I forgive and release ____ (name) unto God.
This person ____(name) is in her/his right place at all times.
I choose freedom for myself; I am free, ____(name) is free.
And so it is!

Forgiveness is the key, a tool, and the first step to Inner Peace.

Eileen Siegel Bowen

VISUALIZATION TOOL

"Your hands are tied in action, but your hands are not tied in imagination – and everything springs forth from the imagination. Everything." ~Abraham *via Esther Hicks*

"We're going to give you a very powerful statement: Everything that you will someday live, in terms of life experience —— and by some day, we mean as soon as right now, tomorrow, the next day, or some day —— anything that you will some day live, you have first imagined. Because nothing will manifest in your experience without the imagination process happening first." ~Abraham

What imaginations are you choosing to allow my friend? Choose with alertness, choose only what you want to manifest in your life.

We use our imagination every moment as the mind travels to distant lands and people. Imagination is the "Creative Energy" of the Universe, and we continue to use it every moment with or without awareness. If, for example, you are going to meet someone, you travel to meet them in your mind even before you are physically there. You imagine telling them the things you want to tell them, and then you meet them and do what you imagined. However, most of the time we are not aware that we have actually met the person energetically in our imagination and then what we imagined, we created in the physical. Any visualization tool is an art of using your imagination consciously and creatively to create what you truly want. Ancient scriptures and writings say that we began as a thought in the mind of God, and then we were created. In imagination there is no task big or small, every task is effortless and when there is conscious awareness in every imagination, then grand creation happens.

In the words of Joseph Campbell:

"The cave you fear to enter holds the treasure you seek. Fear of the unknown is our greatest fear. Many of us would enter a tiger's lair before we would enter a dark cave. While caution is a useful instinct, we lose many opportunities and much of the adventure of life if we fail to support the curious explorer within us."

It takes courage to move within and imagine the impossible – let us be courageous enough to create magic and miracles for ourselves and this Planet.

∞

EXERCISE FOR FORGIVENESS

Create a sacred space for yourself where you will not be disturbed by people, pets, or the telephone.

Sit in a comfortable position, relax your body, take a few deep breaths, and close your eyes.

Now gently turn your attention inside your body, and watch the breath move in and out through your lungs without any effort.

Mentally call toward you the love and light of the Creator, visualize yourself surrounded by a brilliant light within, through, and around you.

Now imagine the person who has hurt you, whom you were not able to forgive.

See yourself and this person communicating with each other in an open, honest and harmonious way.

See yourself and this other person nod, agree, and smile.

Feel within yourself that this mental image is possible, experience it completely as if it is happening now.

You can go a little further and even see both of you hugging each other.

Open your eyes when you feel complete.

Repeat this simple exercise often, as many times as you can throughout your day. Your sincerity in doing this will surely resolve the problem completely.

***It should be noted here that this technique works to dissolve our internal barriers and allow us to flow effortlessly in harmony with life. This technique cannot be used to control the behavior of anyone against their will.

∞

USING THE FORGIVENESS TOOLS

A woman from my neighborhood came to me for healing as she was so stressed by her husband's behavior. She had recently found out that he was having an affair with someone who posed to be her friend.

Her husband had stopped coming home and one day called her on the phone to let her know that he would not be coming back to her anymore.

This lady loved her husband so much, she was very hurt, and she came for a healing for her heart. We discussed about the freedom of love and how it is very important to free oneself and others to help healing to happen.

After our long discussion the woman understood that her relationship with her husband had been one of dependency and control and the moment he walked out of her life, she became extremely angry and saddened. This was also affecting her health for she started suffering from ulcers.

Most of the time, we hold others as prisoners in our life. We believe something about the person in our minds and hold it as true and when the person threatens our belief, we immediately make them our enemy, and we stress and terrorize ourselves over our belief. No one can make us angry or upset, only we have the power to do this to ourselves. And we are also capable and powerful to change our life by deeply looking into and questioning our beliefs.

I gave her the affirmation and visualization exercise to do every day as many times as she needed.

After about 3 weeks, she came to me again. She looked so relaxed and happy, and she said that her ulcers also went away. She told me that as she started to do the affirmations and visualizations sincerely every day, she noticed that she felt so much happier and did not feel the need to wallow in her sadness anymore. Also she was now able to see that if she truly loved her husband, she would have to allow him his freedom.

Two weeks later she told me that a week ago her husband called her and asked her to forgive him. He also said that the woman whom he was with had left him.

It is interesting to note that once we choose to let go of the drama, there is no energy flowing to expand the drama in anyway.

The moment this woman started forgiving and releasing her husband, she stopped creating the drama in her life. Thus, when her energy stopped flowing in that direction, no further creation happened. Therefore, the other woman automatically left as she had been pulled and attracted only to the play of the drama. Once there was no energy feeding the drama, she had to go.

Every relationship in our life is divinely orchestrated, and every situation comes to into our reality for us to anchor greater consciousness. Whether the mind is labeling it as good or bad, every experience you have is allowing you to evolve as a Spiritual being. Each experience is guiding you to become unconditional love and compassion which is your TRUE nature. Everything that you experience today is for your ultimate Highest Good.

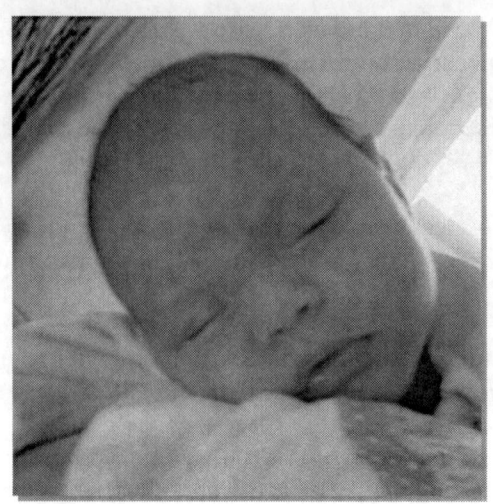

2 BELIEF AND TRUST

"There are two basic motivating forces; fear and love. When we are afraid, we pull back from life. When we are in love, we open to all that life has to offer with passion, excitement, and acceptance. We need to learn to love ourselves first, in all our glory and our imperfections. If we cannot love ourselves, we cannot fully open to our ability to love others or our potential to create. Evolution and all hopes for a better world rest in the fearlessness and open-hearted vision of people who embrace life." ~John Lennon

∞

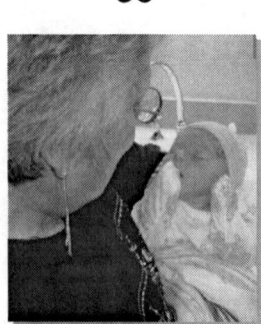

THERE IS A VAST DIFFERENCE BETWEEN BELIEF & TRUST

Belief is intellectual, it involves thinking, and it is a learned conditioning from the outside world: Fear arises out of beliefs.

Trust is created by conscious knowing of truth from within. Trust does not involve thinking as it only needs ones awareness. It is the innocence of a baby who trusts its mother without any doubt: Love arises out of trust.

The mind brings in doubt and when doubts arise, fear also arises as you search for a belief to hold on to. Fear is the most powerful enemy of all. Fear cripples, confuses, and makes one to die many times while alive. The concept of fear arises only in the confused mind, a mind that knows only what it knows, a mind that does not know anything before the body came into existence, and a mind that can ride its vehicle only through the help of the physical senses.

When you put your mind into a belief, you need an organization, laws, dogmas, and commandments; it becomes a system. Any kind of belief system is a hindrance to your spiritual growth, to your potential expansion, and to the gifts that you have brought into this Planet. In a belief system you are never given a chance to explore your Truth. Belief is the easy and most limited way to live your life. Beliefs take you away from your truth by preventing you from exploring the unknown, from creating wonderment through your gifts, and by keeping you inside a box in which your mind believes to be safe.

Your Truth can be known only by your own individual experience. This Universe is teaming with a grand assortment of creation. As each individual is unique, your gifts can be known only by your experience and never by a belief.

> "Truth does not come and go nor shift nor change, in this appearance now and then in that, evading capture and escaping grasp. It does not hide. It stands in open light, in obvious accessibility. It is impossible that anyone could seek it truly, and would not succeed." Lesson 107
> ~*A Course In Miracles*

Trust is not about God or faith. Trust is complete surrender to life from the place of greater Understanding. The greater understanding comes from the heart and never from the mind. The mind is not built for trust or love. The mind is a storehouse of knowledge and experiences; hence, the mind is a grand holding place for beliefs. Emotions arise because of judgment of beliefs as being good or bad. Trust has nothing to do with emotions. Trust is a state of being. It is a feeling of the heart; it is not an emotion. It is referred to as the "gut feeling". The gut feeling is the truth that you are born with; it is your Divine Guidance. When the gut feeling is pleasant, you are on the right path. In contrast, if your gut feeling is not comfortable, the path you have chosen is not for you.

TRUST YOUR FEELINGS BEFORE YOU TRUST ANYONE ELSE. YOUR FEELINGS ARE YOUR DIVINE GUIDANCE. IF ANYTHING MAKES YOU FEEL GOOD, THEN DO IT. IF YOU DO NOT GET A GOOD FEELING, THEN IT IS NOT FOR YOU.

∞

Diana Beardsley
YOU ARE THE RIVER OF LIFE

Gut level feelings are a perfect and clear compass within every human being. One who listens and follows his feelings will be able to effortlessly flow with the river of life.

Love and fear are two sides of a coin. Fear arises out of ignorance, and love arises from the illumination of knowing your Truth. If you feed your fear, you become a slave to worry, doubt, and neediness. And because of your fear, you can be exploited in the hands of the wrong people.

According to the Buddha, "Fear is the original sin." When you are in fear, it is very easy to be exploited. Anyone can convince you to do certain things, make laws, create conditions, and glean a huge harvest from your fears. The belief in unworthiness and lack is easier to enforce when people are in fear. For thousands of years, this is what most of the religions on the Planet have been doing.

Hence, fear moves you to search for security, money, power, fame, and material things. In search of this, greed, selfishness, and cruelty become a norm; you lose your self-respect and become enslaved. Fear makes you to always search on the outside; it will never allow you to go within.

Fear is your indicator – it shows you that you need to illuminate yourself with love. You are in fear because you have no knowledge of who you are, and you only believe about yourself what was told to you by the world outside. Face your fear; do not condemn it. It is a part of your social upbringing. Go beyond it to see what is on the other side. You do not need to fight fear; you only have to understand it.

When you go within, you find that you are the Holy Temple where the Creator resides and that the Holy Scripture is readily available to you.

LIFE is who YOU are. You are the great river of life that flows infinitely. Births, death, and pleasure experiences of the senses are all attractions on the banks of the river of life.

A confused mind attaches itself to the attractions on the banks of the river and does not let go. Fear arises because of attachment, and fear arises because the river of life is flowing while you remain stagnant.

Live life fully each moment. Do not cling to, but enjoy and celebrate the attractions on the banks of this river of life and move on with the flow. For YOU are the river, and YOU are life! The river flows infinitely, and creates amazing magical adventures all through its path. Go as the river, enjoy the magical adventures, and be in the place of excited anticipation of the next moment as you move on.

Diana Beardsley

YOU are the river of life. KNOW the river. GO with the flow.

KNOWING THE CREATOR

"Every mind contains all minds, for every mind is one. Such is the truth. Yet do these thoughts make clear the meaning of creation? Do these words bring perfect clarity with them to you?" ~Lesson 161~ *A Course In Miracles.*

Every soul is embodied with the code of the Creator within, and every soul shall start searching for the Creator in their lifetime. When there is freedom from belief systems, then it is easier to know the Creator through ones experience. However, when society is riddled with belief systems that define and personify a high and mighty Heavenly Father sitting on his throne in the clouds with human personalities of anger and jealousy, we are subject to society's control through our fears of a vengeful God. Such belief systems and religions strive to gain control through fear. Religion has rules and laws that demand a person to pray, sing, chant, fast, or torture themselves with the concept of unworthiness. This is the greatest suffering on the Planet. The concept of unworthiness also portrays man as being sinful and not able to be responsible for his actions. Hence, more organizations like the government, police, courts, and the military are created to supervise the conduct of man. There is nothing bad here. This is just a call for us to wake up to the understanding to live from the heart, and from the place of trust and greater understanding of Our Selves. Everything created has been created only because of agreements. When man agreed to fall in consciousness on the inside, discordance was created on the outside.

The simplest and most profound way to know the Creator is learning to become aware of One's Self. The Self is a part of the Great Divine Presence. Nothing in the Universe can exist without the Divine Presence. Every human, animal, bird, tree, mountain, river, land, air, sky, all beings seen and unseen, and All That Is in the Universe survives only by the essence of the Divine Presence that flows as a great ocean within, through, and around all these forms. Absolutely nothing can ever exist without this Divine Presence. The experience of knowing this creates that which is called TRUST. The only difference between a conscious and unconscious person is that the conscious person knows this and therefore operates from the place of Trust; whereas, the unconscious person does not know this and so he operates from the place of beliefs and fear. Beliefs keep one imprisoned in fear while trust helps one to blossom into his goodness and love. The person who lives from the place of Trust does not need any organization or laws to keep him on the right path. He lives from the connection with the Divine Presence in his heart and he will not be able to commit discord in his life. He does everything with loving intent, and thus his will shall be aligned with God – with the Creator.

When we understand ourselves as a part of the Creator's Divine Presence, trust and surrender become effortless.

There is no need to spend time in rituals and painful processes. You come to know that God is as near to you as your very next breath.

When you start trusting yourself as a part of the Creator's Divine Presence, you experience yourself becoming bigger and bigger in consciousness. Your heart expansion includes everything around you, and everything that comes into your space becomes a part of your loving being; everything – even that which your mind defines as bad.

Accepting the Self, "the good and the bad" within oneself, is the first step toward understanding the Creator. Accepting oneself allows us to accept the good and bad in others also.

Self-acceptance brings immense wisdom, clarity, and understanding. It helps one to see the Greater picture of life. It brings greater understanding about the good and bad in oneself and others. It helps to move out of the judgments of the mind and emerge into the light of understanding.

A person who has self-acceptance is in true self-trust and freedom, this person is able to make good wise decisions, this person does not depend on others for anything, and this person is able to create a joyous reality for his self. Those who have self-esteem and respect for themselves, know how to respect others for they know that no one is better or worse than themselves. They have come to understand that each and every human and each and every created being is precious.

Trust and surrender opens the heart to blossom, and the wisdom of the heart becomes easily accessible. With this trusting, heartfelt openness, we experience ourselves as loving, magnificent beings radiating love and light. We experience our magnificence through every act of love, kindness, forgiveness, and understanding that we extend to every person and situation that is placed in our life. We come to understand life as LOVE, a love that can love the unlovable and forgive the unforgivable.

Being in the radiance of this bliss of LOVE, we come into the KNOWING of the Creator.

∞

GOING BEYOND GOOD OR BAD

According to the TAO, " When people see some things as good, other things become bad."

In this world of duality consciousness, we have practiced our minds to see some things as good and some things as bad. Also the mind has a storehouse of filed ideas and thoughts about good and bad as perceived by our senses and as taught by the society. And we are the Creators and the organizers of this entire play of good or bad. The meaning for everything in life is the meaning we have given it. We are absolutely responsible for our creation. No one else is responsible to make us feel good or bad.

We give meanings to life situations and create judgments. We continue to judge others and ourselves creating pain, stress, and divisions against ourselves and other people. Resistance, comparison, and competition become the theme of everyday situations. We start at a very early age with thoughts of:

"I am not good enough, I cannot be satisfied with myself, I have to be better, bigger, faster, smarter," and the list goes on and on.

Then it plays out with our relationships with other people, other countries, and the world at large. Division occurs and there becomes a huge amount of pain and anguish in the heart.

Life as a human with the mind anchored in judgment creates suffering. The suffering is always because of the perception of good or bad. Running the race is good, but when it is judged as winning or losing, then it becomes suffering. Pain is an experience but when it is judged as bad, it becomes suffering.

The heart is the place of purity, a place where there is oneness, and a place of undivided limitlessness. We are great magnificent beings who chose to keep a tiniest part of ourselves in these human bodies to experience the gift of a human life. We have forgotten our magnificence, and only our heart knows this greater part of our being. Hence, the heart is never compromised by the illusion of judgments of good or bad.

To live in oneness with the heart, brings comfort and peace. To live in oneness with the heart, one has to die. In this contemplation, I am reminded of the verse in the Prayer of St. Francis of Assisi:

"It is in dying that we are born to eternal life."

If you watch people on their deathbeds, they have a radiant smile, they know there is no hope, the decision-making is now out of their hands, and out of their minds. They are experiencing freedom!

The real truth about dying while alive is letting go of all of the divisions of good or bad, going beyond good or bad, going beyond what appears to be, being in a neutral state, and being in a place of choice-less consciousness. It is the art of getting out of the mind, watching the mind, and being a witness.

Just stopping to watch the mind while taking short breaths of awareness, brings greater understanding and helps to drop all illusions of good or bad. For only we are capable of making ourselves suffer by believing our thoughts and by constantly arguing with reality. Thoughts are never personal, they do not stay, they come, and they go. It is our choice to personalize them or not. No person in this world has the power to make us scared, angry, sad, or stressed. Only we have the power to do this to ourselves. Such fear based emotions arise out of personalizing our thoughts and beliefs about the world around us, and they are the insanity of being at war with reality. Let us choose to go beyond the concept of good or bad as we are powerful beings and it is possible for us.

WE HAVE THE POWER TO TRANSFORM OUR LIVES

Have you ever thought about questioning your beliefs?

Your beliefs have the capacity to either destroy you or empower you. Whatever you put your belief on becomes true for you.

How many of us believe certain things and create them again and again in our lives and also ask, "Why is life so hard on me?"

How many times do we repeat in our minds and in our language things like:

"I get a cold at least three times a year – this is the flu season; at age 40 my aunt and my mother had cancer; there is unemployment everywhere; people get old and sick; money is hard to come by; this world is not a safe place; I am a sinner; nobody loves me..."

What are your beliefs today, my friend?

Sit with yourself in silence, take time to note down your thoughts, and use courage to question them. How would your life be without these thoughts? Take each negative thought and think a positive/opposite thought for it. If your thought is "my mother does not love me," think an opposite thought for this, it can be "my mother loves me/I do not love my mother." As you think the opposite thought, find good reasons for the thought, and you will be surprised. You will remember the times that you have not loved your mother, and the times that your mother really went out of her way to do things for you. Then you will realize that the world around you was not crazy; but your beliefs about the world around you made you the crazy one!

It takes real courage to question our thoughts, to accept that we are the creators of our reality, and to realize that no one other than our own selves are responsible for the way things are in our lives. Acknowledging this is the first step to transforming our life to a richer, healthier, and more positive place. When we change our thoughts, things around us automatically change!

Let us choose to give this gift to ourselves, let us choose to sit in meditation with our thoughts, be very aware, and notice that we are powerful beings beyond limitations. We can create the reality we want with what we choose to focus on and to believe.

∞

The Little Fleas – My Teachers

I have a most intriguing experience to share about how I came to understand and trust the Divine Presence within me.

At one time my house was infested with fleas. I did not have pets but these tiny creatures had walked in from next door where there were two dogs and two cats!

These fleas were stinging my family and me so badly. I went to the store to get a flea spray. It did not work; the more I sprayed, the more they got into the whole house, even inside the bed and closets! In desperation, I approached the office of the apartment where I lived and they sent an exterminator to bomb the apartment to get rid of the fleas.

The week the exterminator came it was wonderful; no more fleas!

A friend called and I told her about the fleas, she assured me that they have not left because they lay eggs on the edges of the carpet, and that they will come back. I was disappointed as the minute I hung up the phone, I got stung by the fleas. I was so angry at these little creatures and they annoyed me so much. I could not even have a proper sleep at night because of the stinging and scratching all night long.

I sat down in despair and focused on the fleas. I trusted that they could understand me, I called unto them in my mind's eye, and I asked them why they were doing this. As I was sending these thoughts, slowly my inner being revealed to me my power to speak words of power over any situation in my life! I called out to the guardians of the fleas because I believe that every being is born with its guardian on this planet. So I lined up all of the fleas and their guardians in front of me in my thoughts.

I thanked them for coming to me in this annoying disguise and letting me know that I am powerful and that I can speak words of power. I spoke to them, and I affirmed that my body and my home were my space. I thanked them for letting me know my power, and I wished them well and sent them to their space with love and light. I felt a calm settle over my heart.

In that very moment, the fleas LEFT MY HOME AND NEVER CAME BACK! I now understood the application of this powerful tool. My friend was amazed.

More Teachings

A few years ago, I had planted some wild flowers in my pots, and they bloomed with all the colors and they were so beautiful. One morning, I saw a swarm of green bugs eating away all the buds and the tender shoots. I tried to spray water mixed with a little cooking oil which made the bugs to slip away, but the oil scorched the plants when the sun came up. So I stopped spraying the oil-water, and the bugs came back in large numbers.

My heart reminded me of the tool I used with the fleas, so I sat near the plants and asked the bugs and their guardians to leave.

That same evening, I saw the bugs were still there, but a very strange thing had happened. I was wondering how did so many tiny red flowers appear on my plants and when I took a closer look, they were actually a group of ladybird beetles ravenously eating all the green bugs on the plants. They finished all of the bugs and then left after a week.

The plants became healthy, had so many flowers on them all through the summer, and gave joy to all who passed by that way!

These incidents brought to me the greater truth that we are the power in our life; this is our gift – our birthright from the Divine Presence within us. We have the ability to speak words of power over any situation in our life. The so-called "imperfect situations" are actually blessings-in-disguise to help us to tune into our power. Hence, bless and let go the "fleas-negativity" in your life. They obey to your command when it comes from love and gratitude from within your heart!

BEING CONSCIOUS OF NEEDINESS

"The real fight is in, not there on the outside, and the real fight is not with others. The real fight is with your own unconsciousness, with your own unawareness." ~ Osho

Most of us are unconsciously addicted to neediness. This unconsciousness makes us constantly in need of others' love, approval, reward, recognition, acknowledgement, and attention. In order to get this, we go out of our way to please others and do all that which is not true for us.

We forget how to be ourselves. In our neediness, we strive to do the things that the other person likes; we forget what we like.

We put up with things that our body and mind does not approve of just to satisfy the need of getting the attention of the other person. We easily accept any kind of abuse or humiliation just because of our neediness of the other person's love, or approval.

This unconscious behavior makes every human relationship painful. Then worry, doubt, stress, and anxiety become the norm of everyday life.

We come into this world alone, and we go back alone. We are Divine beings, and our Divinity within is abundant enough to satisfy all of our needs. The problem began when we lost focus on our Divinity within and started focusing on the outside for our needs. Attachment to something outside the self is an illusion. Even if people love each other very much and tend to cling to each other while awake, at some point sleep walks in and takes each one far away to mysterious lands.

When we grow up, our senses start working, and we see that we are alone. As we never trained our senses to go within, we often end up attaching ourselves to people, power, and material things on the outside.

Every indulgence of clinging or neediness on the outside, is a sure sign of forgetting to connect with the Divinity within. Neediness comes out of the fear of being alone.

When we choose to focus, connect, and grow in the Divinity within us, we are doing a great service for ourselves. By focusing on the Divinity within, we become mature, alert, awake, satisfied, loving, and compassionate. We become the wellspring of understanding and wisdom. Our actions and relationships are authentic when they come from the place of the Divinity within. All actions and relationships that arise from the mind and its logic, will be out of neediness. Every action that is not from the place of Divinity within, will automatically seek for approval or reward. It will come from the place of expectation, and expectations lead to disappointments.

When we understand and accept our whole selves from the heart, we radiate with the light of wisdom from within. We can then go beyond need, and we can share our light with others. Otherwise, when we have no light in us, we will become addicted to things on the outside to satisfy. However, the things on the outside can never satisfy us. We will continue to seek and in our seeking, we will not be able to live in our truth. When we do not live in our truth, we lose our joy.

We can help others only when we have helped ourselves first. This brings to me the flight safety instructions on an airplane, which simply say, to first put the oxygen mask on you before helping anyone else, even if it is a child.

Let us choose to identify, to notice our neediness with an open mind, let us catch ourselves in the act of self-sabotage, and change our programming to self-growth and well being.

THE DIVINE ORCHESTRATION OF LIFE

We think that we are this body, thoughts, emotions and personality. But this body is recycled earth, the thoughts are recycled information from the air waves, the emotions are recycled energy, and the personality depends on relationships with people and situations! If this is so, then who are we really?

Science tells us that the cells of our body are destroyed and new cells form every day. Every day we wake up with a new body. We experience birth and death everyday through our cells, our thoughts and opinions and our experiences. We are not able to touch our two-year-old or ten-year-old body now.

Deepak Chopra, M.D. states that ninety-eight percent of our cells in our body have been completely replaced in less than twelve months with entirely new cells. We are energetically one with everything from a tree in Africa to a squirrel in Siberia. We are one with the planet, the universe, and All That Is. We are our consciousness and our bodies are made of that Divinely universal energy.

The records about "near death experiences" and every ancient wisdom show us that we are not this body; however, we are the consciousness that resides in the body. This body is a beautiful vehicle that helps us to perceive the physical world and gather wisdom from our experiences. Fear and neediness arise only when we think that we are this body and that we need to do everything in our power to help this body and personality-identity to survive. This is the deep unconscious sleep that humanity is afflicted with. Awakening from this sleep is the responsibility of every human being. When enough number of humans are willing to awaken, there will be a grand creation of harmony and peace in the collective human reality.

In Mahayana Buddhism, the Buddha explains the truth about Reality:

> "While any experience certainly seems real enough to us, it's only where we direct our attention while we're having a feeling about the object of our focus that a possible reality becomes that REAL experience."

In other words, what we experience as everyday reality is a form of a collective dream.

Modern quantum theory, which is the most successful of all creations on this Planet, says that the properties of a particle do not even exist until there is an observer to witness it. So it is more clear when the ancient texts say that this world began as a thought in the mind-consciousness of the Creator.

In the words of Deepak Chopra:

"Our brains are too slow to register that every concrete object is winking in and out of existence at the quantum level thousands of times per second."

That includes us, Deepak Chopra continues. If we could perceive what we experience in those moments out of existence, we would never worry about anything again.

In the words of Gregg Braden:

"All that exists is consciousness. Within the consciousness of All That Is, both the world of form and the formless result from a special subjective imagination."

According to John Wheeler, a scientist at Princeton University, we live in a Participatory Universe. Our act of focusing our consciousness is an act of creation in and of itself. We are simultaneously the catalyst for the events of our lives as well as the experiences of what we create. Both are happening at the same time.

Physicists refer to matter as energy that pulsates in different wavelengths. Our body is energy that is denser, our mind is also energy but not so dense. When we go within and bring awareness to the Self, we experience consciousness which is also energy but in a more subtle, purer form. When the body and mind work united with consciousness, then the Divine Presence is felt in oneself and in all beings. The Divine Presence is not the totality of body, mind, and consciousness. The Divine Presence is when the body, mind, and consciousness come together in unity, and it is felt as the infinite being that holds all of existence. The experience of the Divine Presence is very personal; it arises as feelings from the heart, and it cannot be logically explained by the mind in anyway. Each person has to go through this experience to know the Divine Presence. When we come to this experience, we know deep in our being that we are a part of this infinite Divinity who experiences itself through us. By being awakened, we participate consciously in every act of living, we become the witness of life, and the Divine Presence becomes the Ultimate witness.

One of my spiritual teachers, Mooji, asks people in all of his discourses to contemplate on this one question,

"Can the perceiver be perceived?"

This question is not to be answered from the mind. The experience of contemplation of this question, takes one deeper within into an awakened state of consciousness.

When you awaken you live as the GOD WITHIN and your creations come from the place of harmony and peace.

OUR RESPONSIBILITY

Let us wake up to this truth that our reality is Divinely Orchestrated. This is a perfect space created by perfect Divine Orchestration. The only imperfection that can be seen is from the mind. The mind that was created for a specific job; to preserve the body from damage and destruction. The mind takes its protectiveness very seriously and works overtime by putting us inside a box of beliefs thus creating fear to keep our bodies safe. It is our responsibility to comfort our mind by questioning and bringing in understanding. We are completely responsible for what we have created and for what we will continue to create. If we do not like what we see in our reality, it is time for us to take the responsibility of cleaning our thoughts, words, and actions consciously.

> "Words do not teach at all. It is life experience that brings you your knowing. But when you hear words that are a vibrational match to the knowing that you have accumulated, then sometimes it is easier for you to sort it all out."
> ~Abraham

Just As Carl Jung said:

> "Everything that irritates us about others can lead us to an understanding of ourselves."

The world is our Teacher. Every person mirrors to us our unconscious self. The enemy outside mirrors to us the enemy within. If we consciously choose to be present in body, mind, and consciousness, we will be able to realize that every person or situation that makes us angry is actually showing us the things within us that we have failed to reconcile. It takes courage to ask the question:

"What in me has made this angry person or this hopeless situation come into my space?"

Only the mind that is open to being questioned can take this journey. The tragedies in our life almost always have the origin inside of us. As a collective consciousness of humanity, we have collected amazing amounts of data by judgments. Everything that plays around us is our consciousness focusing on the data; data about people, places, things, situations, and everything on the Planet absolutely.

Dr. Ihaleakala Hew Len brings to us a profound view of Ho'oponopono; an ancient Hawaiian practice of reconciliation and forgiveness. He recommends that each one of us take 100% responsibility of cleaning our data. The moment that thoughts arise about people or places, we should consciously tell the data these four things:

> "I LOVE you; THANK you for showing up and letting me know;
> I am SORRY for what is going on in me that is making me see these things in this way; PLEASE forgive."

Furthermore, the moment we bring-in this awareness, the data is erased. We return to zero point, which is pure source, the place where we originated, the kingdom, and the nothingness. From the zero point it is easier for us to see the world with the eyes of a child; to live in wonderment and to create in joy.

Responsibility is the ability to respond to life situations from our heart. The first act of empowering ourselves is accepting responsibility for our life. It means taking responsibility for our happiness, for our health, and for our wisdom. We are born with all of these tools and we need not search for them on the outside. Spending time in silence, connecting with nature, choosing to question our beliefs, asking for guidance from the inner being, energizing our imagination, intending to keep ourselves healthy and relaxed, and empowering our ability to laugh with good hearted innocence at our own creations are wonderful ways of being responsible.

We as humanity are a collective consciousness. We create from this collective as everything on the Planet happens from the output of energy from every single person on this Planet; therefore, we cannot blame anyone – government, politics, religion, or education systems anymore for what is happening around us. People and situations come into our life for us to co-create greater understanding and greater solutions. Everything helps in our expansion as conscious beings. If we hold on to belief systems and play the blame game we will remain stagnant, and we will continue to create that which we do not want.

We are in this Planet at this time to create the new consciousness, a consciousness that creates a New Earth of love, joy, peace, harmony, and wellbeing. We are totally responsible to create this. It starts with us, we need to erase and let go all of our data about others and ourselves.

We do live in a "participatory universe" and our true purpose is to participate 100% in the co-creation of Heaven on Earth.

∞

TRUE FREEDOM

Life flows through you; life moves you all of the time. Everything flows and nothing stays fixed.

When life moves you, move with it; do not place roadblocks of judgment or fear. Your fear and judgment are roadblocks on the easy path that life has chosen for you. Fear is an illusion and it is bondage. When you understand that all is good; you can live in Freedom.

Life always shows you what is good in a more clear and efficient way than you would possibly discover for yourself. Life always works with you and for you; it gets to know the dream in your heart. The thoughts and dreams that you have nourished create a grand energy that wants to create a new paradise for you.

When you need to move toward your dream, life prepares a way for you. You need to leave your comfort zone and flow with the way life leads you. Do not resist as resisting creates more stress and sorrow. Life always has a purpose, and the purpose is toward goodness for all. Move with life, for you do not know the bigger picture – you do not even know what is good for you or for anyone else.

The ability to live from the place of *consciousness, alertness, awareness, and responsibility* is true freedom. It brings in the realization that there is no one out there to control you; you are free to live your life the way you choose.

I have noticed that when there is a law given, people tend to go against it. There was a rule in my son's high school that chewing gum is not allowed in the classroom. The students started to chew gum secretly and my son said that when you put your hand under the desk or chair, you would find innumerable chewed gums stuck underneath. Then they dropped this rule in school, and no one bothered to chew gum in class anymore.

I am reminded of the words of the TAO:

"Try to make people moral, and you lay the groundwork for vice."

Forgetting our Divine Nature is the only illusion on this Planet. We have burdened ourselves so much by the walls of laws, rules, governments, and religions by thinking that we are not good enough. We are born good; we need not strive to be good. Goodness is our Nature. We are a part of the Creator, and every part of the Creator is magnificent and beautiful like the Creator itself. Every human is precious in the eyes of the Creator.

Let us choose to create a world of true freedom; freedom begins by processing our fears. If we turn fear around, only love remains. Love is all that is real. LOVE IS ALL THAT IS.

Let us choose to trust and live in love. Let us teach our future generations to live in love, to grow in self-esteem and self-worth, and to learn to trust in themselves. It is time we recognized and remembered our Divine Nature.

It is time to wake up the Buddha qualities – the Christ qualities within us. These qualities are True for every human being as every human heart is made of this material.

When we choose to live from trust, we raise our vibration. By each person's higher vibration, the collective vibration of humanity becomes higher, and we create *Heaven on Earth*.

∞

SPIRITUAL TOOLS TO WORK WITH

AFFIRMATIONS

The word "I AM" represents the Grand Divine Presence. Whenever we use the phrase I AM in a sentence, we are agreeing with whatever we say, and we give our will for it to happen. Therefore, take notice of what are you are focusing your "I AMs" on.

My neighbor next door continues to say:

"I am a plant killer; I kill all my plants."

I am amused in seeing that she buys plants, does not take care of them, they die, she throws them away, then goes to buy more to do the same, and continues to affirm to everyone that she kills her plants. This is an example of unconscious creation.

When we become conscious of the Divine within us, we empower ourselves with conscious use of the word "I AM" in our thoughts and our words.

These are many affirmations that you can work with everyday to empower your conscious connection with the Divine Presence. Affirmations can be done anytime, anywhere, but they have to be done with feeling. Also a specific time and space can be created everyday for repeating any one of the affirmations that you feel would help you at the time.

I am worthy.
I am good at what I do.
I am beautiful.
I am bountiful.
I get better and better every day.
I am healthy and happy.
I am in my right weight now.
I am surrounded by love.
I am divinely protected and guided.
I radiate love and happiness.
I have the perfect job; I love what I do.
I am successful in whatever I do.
I am a wise being.
I am whole and complete.
I am strong and powerful.

I am a loving person.
I love money, money flows to me in avalanches of abundance.
I am capable.
I am peaceful.
I am in my Presence.

These are all positive affirmations for everyday. You can choose one or combine or create one for yourself with the power of the word "I AM" according to the situation you are dealing with. The affirmations are always for the now, in the present tense. The affirmations become powerful and active only when you bind them with your feelings. Choose the sentences you want to be true in your life and say them with feeling. The stronger your intention and feeling, the more faster will be the results.

∞

GROUNDING AND CONNECTING TO THE CENTER OF YOUR HEAD

The grounding meditation strengthens our connection to Mother Earth. We get anchored and nourished by the earth as we go about our daily activities.

The centering meditation helps one to live from the place of their wisdom and unique psychic abilities, which they have brought to this Planet.

Grounding

Sit in a straight back chair, place feet flat on the floor, and close your eyes. Notice your breathing, breathe from your belly, notice your belly expand with every in-breath, and contract with every out-breath. Continue to breath in this manner. Now in your mind's eye imagine a cord of light from the base of your spine extending down to the heart of the Earth. Follow this cord in your imagination from the base of your spine down into the earth, traveling down through the soil, rocks, underground rivers, minerals, until the cord reaches the molten center, the core of the earth and gets anchored.

Do this simple meditation in the mornings and know that this cord keeps you solidly anchored and connected to the Planet, so that you will not be swayed by the push and pull of discord around you.

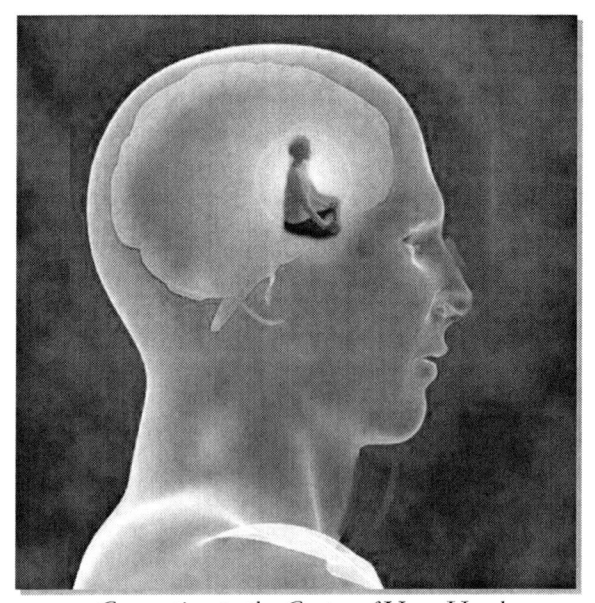

Connecting to the Center of Your Head

Sit in a straight back chair, place your feet flat on the floor, and close your eyes. Notice your breathing, breathe from your belly, notice your belly expand with every in-breath, and contract with every out-breath. Continue to breathe in this manner.

Use both index fingers and touch your temples on either side. Notice where your fingers touch, and draw an imaginary line between the two points. Now move your hands 90 degrees to the right and touch the back of your head and forehead with your index fingers. Note the two points and draw another imaginary line intersecting the first line. Find the point where these lines intersect; this is the center of your head. Now remove your fingers and place your awareness in this place. You will definitely feel something here. This is because this is our place of power.

We gave away our power a long time ago. As we were growing up, we wanted the love and support of the people around us, and in order to please them, we gave away our power. We did all that they asked us to do, and stopped listening to ourselves on the inside.

In the words of my teacher, Jim Self:

"This place of power has been occupied by - father, mother, teacher, and minister all our life. It is not that they were good or bad, but that they had expectations that you fulfill, they thought that they were doing the best for you according to them."

Because you needed their love, you allowed them to take your power. Now, in the center of your head they reside and they still dictate their opinions to you with which you act in everyday situations. You may sometimes have the feeling:

"I deal with this situation like my father did, I talk just like my teacher, or my mother did not like cabbages so I do not like them also, etc."

Your situations are not theirs, and your experiences cannot be their experiences. You are born with divine guidance and wisdom gifted to you by your Father/Mother God; it is time to anchor the wisdom of your soul.

When you place your awareness on the center of your head, every person who had taken residence there has to leave immediately.

Take time to be in the center of your head with eyes closed and also try it with eyes open. As you are placing your awareness on the center of your head continue to breathe gently. Be aware of your center and also be aware of your breath.

Stay in the center with your eyes closed, observing your breath, open your eyes and see the world from the center of your head using your eyes as windows. You can even be more imaginative by seeing yourself as a tiny figure sitting on a beautiful chair in the center of your head.

Begin walking around with your awareness focused on the center of your head. Be in the center of your head while talking to people and notice the difference.

Use this powerful tool many times during the day, walk your life with your awareness placed on the center of your head. This is your sanctuary and your place of power; you can do all your energy work from there with peace and harmony. This is possible and it works like magic.

∞

A Prayer from ~Marianne Williamson

    Sit with your eyes closed for two minutes. During that time, pray to be shown images of yourself embodying the highest, more creative possibility for your life. See yourself radiant, experiencing fully both power and joy. Embrace these images – allow them to settle in, to align with your heart, to lock in to your consciousness. And then repeat these words, "There is no order of difficulty in miracles. In God, all things are possible." And so it is. Amen.

∞

Eileen Siegel Bowen
3 ALLOWING AND SURRENDER

"Always say "yes" to the present moment. What could be more futile, more insane, than to create inner resistance to what already is? What could be more insane than to oppose life itself, which is now and always now? Surrender to what is. Say "yes" to life — and see how life suddenly starts working for you rather than against you."
~Eckhart Tolle

∞

EVERYTHING IS CREATED FOR YOU

Yes! Every created thing on this Planet is for you to enjoy and share from the place of celebration. But the human mind whose only concern is about the survival of the body, does not understand these things. It is always on the look out to possess things that enhance the body's survival. Humans as a collective, have chosen to live from the mind and accept the stories of the mind to be real; therefore, we see much chaos and confusion around us. In our confusion, we continue to strive for money, power, and possessions. In our striving, we become blind to our natural self which is unconditional love, joy, peace and harmony. Everything that is other than our natural self becomes stress.

Striving for money, power and possessions is an illusion. Death of the physical body arrives and takes them all away reminding us that we cannot possess anything in this physical world. We are here only to experience the love and joy of creation. Awakening comes for some at the time of death, which becomes too late, as they realize that they were given everything but they chose to be blind. Busy in their striving for possessions, they forgot to live and celebrate their lives.

Passionately living life moment-by-moment with alertness and awareness, reveals the grand gifts of existence. The only goal of existence is living life completely and enjoying the gifts that every moment brings. There is no other goal other than living life itself. We are a part of existence; we cannot be separate. The more in tune we are with existence, the more alive we become. The mind was created to protect the body; but we are not the body and neither are we the mind. The body and the mind are tools for us to live and enjoy life with from the place of unconditional love, harmony, peace and joy. Choosing to live only from the mind keeps us very limited and in a place of stress and fear. The body, which is an amazing tool of creation, is not able to bear this stress and thus it creates messages of disease and discomfort.

∞

Eileen Siegel Bowen

THE ACT OF SURRENDERING

Surrendering comes from choosing to live from the place of our wholesome selves. It is choosing to live in Oneness; it is merging our will with the will of the Creator. The will of the Creator IS eternal goodness, and our soul and spirit are already one with the eternal goodness. When we live from the place of this oneness, we live life totally and completely while gathering wisdom and knowledge of all the wondrous mysteries and miracles that life bestows on us.

Surrender comes from trust in the Divine and trust in oneself. The meaning of the word surrender in the dictionary is to lose control or to give up. Spiritually, the word surrender means to let go of who you think you are in your mind, and to live from the truth of who you really are. Who you are is a divine embodiment of infinite possibilities. Living from the mind and its stories of the past and future, you become oblivious to these possibilities.

You are a grand creation and everything around you is created for you. Creation happened with you in mind. There is nothing created against you; everything is for you. You cannot have enmity unless you hold an attachment to a belief in your mind and perceive the person or situation to oppose your belief. The world is in the NOW, but you get lost in the world of stories of the past, the future, the world of thoughts, concepts, projections, and opinions. It is very painful to live in a separate mind-created world full of fear, stress, and apprehensions.

The mind is not bad as the mind only knows what it knows. It only knows and holds data collected through the physical senses from the time of birth till now. The mind is an amazing tool that was created to protect the body at all times. The mind took it upon itself to overwork. The mind has no knowledge of anything other than what it knows about the physical you. But you are not only your body and mind. You are an unlimited spirit and an eternal magnificent being of immense potential for expansion in infinite ways. Only when you let go of controlling through your mind's stories, will you be able to allow the potentials of the eternal you to unfold. And since the world around you is your reflection, your unfolding potentials will create greater beauty and grandness on this Planet.

∞

THE SWEETNESS OF SURRENDER

We are eternal beings capable of infinite expansion. We travel beyond time and space. We have focused our energies for our expansion on this Planet at this time. This planet is one of the many way-stations in our soul journey. We come into this Planet well equipped to gather wisdom through our experiences. We bring a miniscule part of our grand essence into a physical body for experience here. The mind was created to protect the body and hence it continues to collect data from the time the physical body comes into existence.

We listen to the mind and its data every day, and we habituate ourselves to run on autopilot thus placing our trust entirely on our mind. This means that we have literally fallen asleep. We have fallen asleep to our wholesome selves.

Since the mind gets overworked and overwhelmed, it constantly brings messages from the place of fear. The mind thinks that the world is not a safe place. The mind can connect only from the data it has collected from its beliefs and perceptions about the outside world. Hence it only knows what it knows. It does not know about the eternal soul or this beautiful life journey of conscious expansion. If we continue to give the mind the responsibility of running our lives, we find life to be in chaos and confusion.

It is the responsibility of every human to awaken to the magnificence and splendor of their eternal, wholesome selves. As pointed out earlier, reality or life has been created for us, and reality will constantly push us into intense situations that trigger us to awaken to the TRUTH OF WHO WE ARE.

We see examples of this sometimes where excellence happens in extreme situations – where ordinary people perform extraordinary acts when they find themselves in unusual life threatening situations. Such as a person who saves a child from the clutches of a wild river and finds that it was the first time he ever attempted to swim, the extraordinary acts of people who run fearlessly into a burning building to save a loved one, and so forth. Apparently, reality made these people to suddenly let go of their fear-beliefs. They opened to the wholesomeness of who they truly are and thereby performed these extraordinary feats.

There is an ancient practice in Tibet where a lama who is seeking enlightenment is made to run fast on the jagged edges of the mountain without stopping even if he is tired. At the most extreme point, the mind lets go and the Spirit takes over and the lama experiences his wholesome self. Even athletes who run marathons experience this grand moment of letting go and allowing their spirit to take over at the moment their body and mind can no longer go on. They enjoy the experience of this spiritual expansiveness so much that they want to run again and again, and they are unable to explain what happened. These examples show that humans are not small, helpless, or limited in anyway. The only problem is that we fall asleep to our magnificence. We create stories and movies of imaginary superheroes and admire them, and we forget to recognize the greatness within ourselves.

At one time I experienced the enormous pain of living from this mind-created world. When my children were very young, they were often sick. I was so worried that I lost myself in fear every time a sickness appeared. On one of the visits with the doctor my little girl was delirious with fever. The queue of patients was so huge and they would not move fast. I was also so tired from my long day at work. The extremity of the situation broke something in me. I dropped all of my mind-created fears and beliefs about the doctor, my daughter's sickness, the medicines, taking control of the situation, etc., and etc. There was no more desire in me for anything, and I became tired of my fears. Suddenly, I realized that I was only her physical mother. The life-giving Spirit part of my daughter did not come from me, it had come from the Divine. I left without seeing the doctor and went home with my daughter. Surprisingly, her fever left her and she became well!

This revelation for my sleeping consciousness was mind-blowing and that was the moment I surrendered. I understood that if I, being a human, can give so much for the child I bore physically, then how much would the Divine, whom gave the child its Spirit and Life, give for its child. I realized that I had to remove my fearful, controlling, and clinging self out of the way for my daughter's Divine Parent to takeover. This act of removing myself from blocking life's path with my mind-created fear has brought immense healing, excellence, success, peace, and harmony for my family and me.

The joy and excitement I felt in this sweet surrender makes me to choose to be alert and awake in every situation. My stress is my indicator. If at any moment there is stress, anxiousness, or expectation, I am amused to note that my mind had been busy taking control of situations with fear stories.

It is not necessary to go to the place of extreme situations for us to let go or surrender. Nothing ever belonged to us to cling to or attach to in any way. The concept of belong or possess exists only in the mind-created story of a past or a future. Our wholesome self is already ONE with the eternal goodness, and there is nothing we need at any given time. Reality is so benevolent that what IS in front of us NOW is enough and more than what we would need.

The act of surrender simply means that you trust reality as your friend, you live from the place of allowing and acceptance, you live without stress, there is nothing to do, no one to be, and no place to go. We lose our entire mind-created world yet we gain our freedom, our Oneness, and our truly close connection to the Divine. We accept life as it is and exist in the place of excited anticipation of the gifts each moment brings. As we continue to live from this place of conscious awareness, this world becomes a kinder and wondrously beautiful place.

∞

WORRYING IS SENDING NEGATIVE PRAYER

"If I could tell the World just one thing it would be, we're all okay. And not to worry because worry is wasteful and useless in times like these."
~Jewel Kilcher, *Hands*

Loving and worrying cannot occupy the same space. They are two opposing frequencies. There are people who say, "I love my husband so much that I worry about him, or I worry about my children a lot."

Loving is not an emotion. Loving is complete trust that all is well.

Worrying does not help anyone. On the contrary, it makes things even harder for the person who is facing a tough situation. We are energy beings, and we are energetically connected to each other beyond space and time. Our thoughts, feelings, and words bind each other energetically, and this is how prayers (both negative and positive) work.

Worrying, IS sending negative prayer. Worrying is so harmful that it will keep a person stuck in the negative situation that they are in. By worrying about someone, we are sucking away the person's energy, and we are sending a negative prayer by affirming their weakness. Whenever we have worry thoughts about our loved ones, it is wise to understand that these thoughts of ours are not going to help them or us in any way.

Worry or sadness arise from the argument with reality. Every argument creates greater suffering. The suffering is always from the mind, and it has nothing to do with the person or the situation. In the greater play of life, since the mind does not even know what is good for ourselves or for anyone else, then why would we bring our mind stories to argue, defend, or create war inside us against reality?

When we create discord on the inside, the world immediately mirrors our discord. The moment we go into this space, we deplete our life-force energy – the energy that helps our body and mind to function. We stop thinking clearly and our low energy seeks to balance by sucking this life-force energy from others. Yes, and even from those whom we are worrying about. We remain oblivious to our capacity to create healing and harmony. When we stop believing and attaching to our thoughts, we step into peace.

I have noticed and experienced that when I rewrite my worry thoughts with life affirming thoughts, I come to peace and harmony. Miraculously, the person to whom I am sending life affirming thoughts, also finds healing solutions to their problems. Witnessing our thoughts and rewriting them with our loving visualization and affirmation is a sweet surrender and a most powerful way of bringing the LIGHT of consciousness into our everyday life.

Send those who are facing a tough situation positive life affirming thoughts like:

"You can make it, you are getting better and better, you are always Divinely guided and protected."

See this person in your mind's eye smiling, happy, and healthy. Ask for Divine love and light to cover them, protect them, and bring positive solutions for the highest good of all concerned. Choosing life affirming thoughts over worrying creates miracles for both the giver and the receiver.

I have also noticed that when I chose to disengage from my mind-created discord, the people around me also began to lose their discord and live from the place of clarity.

∞

BEING FULLY PRESENT

Many of us worry about the future a lot. Worrying about the future, keeps you in mind-controlled planning of the future, and the future never comes. Even that which is your future, can only become this now moment. If you are lost in the mind story of a future, you have missed YOU in this moment. For you live in this world of the NOW, not a past or a future world. Do not forfeit the gifts of the present moment for some unknown future that never comes.

Surrender involves bringing Presence into every aspect of life. Surrender is the acceptance of your total Self – body, mind, spirit, and soul. It is vital to acknowledge and collect the missing pieces of "you" in this "now" moment. You are giving the gift of your total Presence to you in this now moment as you are born with amazing gifts and capabilities. You can realize this only when you are fully present here with what is here. Being fully present, you feel the presence of everything around you. You can feel this universe teaming with life and bringing in powerful messages for you.

When you are fully present, you can feel the Divine Presence filling the space between all things. So when you are in Presence, you are powerful, and you are in Oneness. The Present moment reveals the eternal, the Oneness as the world of thoughts, concepts, the past, religions, traditions, and opinions absolutely dissolve in the Presence of this Oneness.

"God is not in heaven – God is in the present moment. If you are also in the present moment, you enter the temple." ~Osho

Intelligence is not about planning a future, or problem solving, or aiming for a goal. Intelligence is the capacity to understand that there is no past as it is only a memory, and there is no future for it is only an imagination. Intelligence is to be awake, alert, and fully present in this moment. Each moment of life brings in a new gift, and unless you are aware and alert, you will miss it and not be able to enjoy it.

When living from the mind, we continue to react to life situations mechanically and sometimes, on autopilot mode. When we live from the place of being alert and aware, we respond to situations rather than react to them. Life situations can bring emotions of anger, jealousy, fear, sadness, and so forth. These emotions are due to attachment to thoughts and opinions. The thoughts hit the mind about the situation or person and create opinions. But when we choose to be alert and aware, we watch our thoughts, choose to go beyond them, and we do not blindly react and thus regret our actions.

Our awareness allows us to watch the emotions. When we are fully present watching the emotions, a greater transformation happens. It is surprising to note that whatever emotions arise, they immediately dissolve in the presence of our Oneness – our wholesome self. Emotions do not have power over us; we are the power in our life. So in awareness, let us allow things to express and surprise us. Let us be present to accept, relax, and not put our emotions on thinking that something is wrong. Only by being present do we come to Oneness.

"Something amazing happens when we surrender and just love. We melt into another world, a realm of power already within us. The world changes when we change. The world softens when we soften. The world loves us when we choose to love the world." ~Marianne Williamson

If we do not surrender to the truth of who we are, then we have to create an illusory world from the mind. A world that makes us to constantly not stand in our truth. A world that requires us to please, to prove, and to perform to others in order to get an illusory support from the outside world. We then find out that the world can never be our friend as the world is only our projection of our wants and needs from identifying ourselves as just a body. This keeps us small, limited, and in constant fear. Without the story about our self as a body to survive, we realize that our very nature is pure joy and excitement. Hence choosing to surrender is not to reach any enlightened state, but to be in the place of our joy and excitement. When we live from this place, we attract all the circumstances and opportunities that bring more and more of this joy and excitement into our space. Then the world outside, which is our mirror, has no other choice but to support us.

∞

THE ART OF WATCHING THOUGHTS

It is important to know about thoughts before doing any kind of work on oneself. The thoughts that come to our mind are from the air waves and not from us.

Ninety-nine percent of the time, the thoughts we think are not our own as thoughts are poured into the air waves by every human being. Thoughts are just like passing clouds, and they do not stay. We are the infinite sky where the thought clouds pass. It is our choice either to bind our emotions with the passing clouds or just to let them pass. It takes practice to watch the thoughts with awareness and allow them to pass. We do not need to let go of thoughts, because the moment we do not believe them, they let go of us.

In India, there is a practice where special prayers are done during the time of the "Brahma Muhurta" or the Hour of God. The Brahma Muhurta is during the very early morning hours before sunrise – between three and four 'o clock in the morning. The Vedic seers discovered that it is the most auspicious time for prayer and meditation. It is a time when many are asleep and still in the world of dreams, they have not entered into their daily restless thoughts, and so no thoughts are being poured into the air waves. Nature is calm and quiet which helps to meditate and visualize intentions.

We are connected to the collective and we constantly absorb each other's thoughts and think that they are ours. Have you ever had a feeling where you were so happy going about your way and suddenly you meet someone who was not in a good mood? Just by being with them, your thoughts have changed, and you feel down. This is a classic example of how easily we get into each other's space.

We are energy beings and we constantly merge and play into each other's energies because we are not conscious or alert. Thoughts cannot be stopped but spiritual tools can help us to be conscious, alert, and be in the freedom to create our reality without chaos and confusion from thoughts that do not belong to us.

The mind loves to attach to thoughts, to play the game of telling stories – stories about people, places, situations; never-ending stories. If you sit and watch the mind and its stories, they are filled with so many judgments creating a whole new world of suffering.

The moment we watch our mind, we realize that we are not our thoughts, they do not belong to us, and that the thoughts come and they go. It is always our choice not to attach to them. It is always our choice to live in true freedom. Freedom is giving the gift of kindness to oneself, and it means never allowing fear, anger, or sadness to cloud your life. A quiet mind realizes that no belief is true. A quiet mind is True Freedom.

∞

SPIRITUAL TOOLS TO WORK WITH

Along with the grounding and centering exercise of the previous chapter there are two simple tools that can help us to be in the place of True Freedom to create our reality as we want it to be.

Breath Meditation

According to the spiritual teacher, Eckhart Tolle, "One conscious breath is meditation."

When you watch your breathing, thoughts automatically disappear. Observing your breath helps you to be present in the present moment, it stills your mind, and thoughts lose their power.

Sit comfortably and close your eyes. Take a few moments to simply be. Notice whatever is being experienced in the moment; it may be sounds, physical sensations, thoughts, or feelings. Without trying to do anything about it, continue like this a little while, allowing you to settle down.

Now, bring your attention to the breath. Simply notice the breath moving in and out as the body inhales and exhales. Notice how the breath moves in and out automatically and effortlessly.

Start noticing all of the details of this breathing experience. The feeling of the air moving in and out of the nose, the way the belly rises and falls, and the way the entire body moves as it breathes.

The mind will wander away from the breath, that happens sometimes, and that is okay. That is a part of the meditation itself. When you notice that you are no longer observing the breath, gently bring your attention back to it.

Let all of your experiences, your thoughts, emotions, and bodily sensations come and go in the background of this awareness of the breath. Notice how all of your thoughts, emotions, bodily sensations, and awareness of sounds and smells, come automatically and effortlessly like the breath.

When you practice this exercise consistently everyday for ten minutes, it will be easier to become aware of the tendencies of your mind when you are not in meditation. This awareness creates the possibility for the mind to let go of attachment to thoughts in everyday life.

∞

Premlatha Rajkumar
THE MIRACLE LIGHT PRAYER

This mode of prayer is powerful and magical. I have been doing this prayer from the time of when I was very young. Through this prayer, I felt closer and more connected with the heart of the Creator, and also I found I could manifest the things that I wanted in my life.

For a long time, I had been sharing it with friends, helping them when they had problems, and then I was sharing this with people who came for healing. I have witnessed the amazing power of this prayer in my life and in the lives of people who learnt this technique.

This is not a complicated prayer, and it involves no words. It helps one to merge with the will of the Creator which is a grand act of surrendering.

When I was young, I felt that this mode of prayer would definitely empower people who were going through tough situations. For a long time, I was sharing this by word of mouth. And only a few years ago, I put it into words.

At one time, I understood that sharing your miracles with people and helping them to understand and connect with their Divine gifts within, is the greatest gift to give to humanity. I believe that true service is in showing people their power and all of the riches that they are born with.

I am reminded of the proverbial saying, "Give a man a fish and you feed him for a day; show him how to catch fish, and you feed him for a lifetime." In this way, the Miracle Light Prayer is an empowerment for your lifetime.

The Miracle Light Prayer is all about aligning yourself with your family of light. Your family of light is your Spiritual Kingdom within that includes your Higher Self, your angels, guardians, and your guides that are born with you to help you in this planet. They are always around you and ever ready to help you in any way. But it is only when you call unto them that they will be able to help you because they are bound by human freewill.

The most important thing to do when coming into the Spiritual kingdom within, is to keep your body (the cup) empty (empty of all worries and fear). This way, the Love and Light of the Creator can pour and fill in you. The Great Spirit of the Creator is powerful, blinding, liquid, golden white light. The Creator's Spirit breathed into you when you were made. Every breath you take is God.

We are co-creators with the Great Spirit of the Creator on this planet.

To communicate with Spirit you do not need a language. All you need are your feelings. And the most important, are your feelings of worthiness. You are worthy to receive and be blessed with great and wondrous things.

To begin the communication, please create a sacred space for yourself in your home where you will not be disturbed by people, pets or the telephone. You can create an altar, it is not that Spirit desires for you to do rituals to communicate, but it is just a mark of respect for yourself and for Spirit.

To create an altar, you can bring a few fresh flowers, light a candle, place clear water in a clear crystal bowl, you can place pictures of loved ones, any ornaments, or small stones or crystals. Anything that you feel is close to your heart, can make up your altar.

Sit in front of your altar, go to the center of your head, and visualize in your mind's eye, your body as an empty jar or cup waiting to be filled with the love and light of Great Spirit. And see in your mind's eye, the huge blinding, brilliant, liquid, golden-white light, of the Creator – like a sun above your head.

Observe your breathing. With every in breath, pull down this liquid, golden-white light from the crown of your head to flow into your body and fill your body. As you breathe out allow this light to overflow out to the space around you through your heart.

Continue to breathe in this manner of filling with liquid, golden-white light from your crown by visualization. As every cell of your body gets rejuvenated with love and light, you will feel peace, harmony, and even a chill may run up your spine. At this time, you understand that you are in Oneness with your Spiritual Kingdom within. Your will is the Creator's will! And the Creators will is eternal Goodness.

At this place of love and light, bring to your mind your petition, or your feeling of need. In your mind's eye, with your powerful thoughts and feelings, see your happy goal (the happy result to your need that you want to achieve). See and feel deep within your being the happy result only. See yourself smiling and in great joy as you are in the place of this perfect result. (I have to remind you here that in your Spiritual Kingdom within, there is no time and space. There is only the NOW moment, and so it is enough for you to see only the result in this now moment).

Trust that Spirit knows how to achieve the result. For Spirit's ways are wonderful and more than we can ever imagine or think of. On your part, see only the happy result and give thanks. Give thanks that you are in the place where it is already done. This is the enchantment of faith, and faith is beyond human understanding.

If you have more than one petition, you can bring them to Spirit's presence and do the same by visualizing only the happy result or goal.

After you are done with these things, ask for spiritual protection in the form of this golden white light. Envision it as a huge bubble around you throughout the day. Give gratitude, and open your eyes when you are comfortable.

This beautiful, Spiritual protection light is around you all of the time so you can breathe in lung full's of it wherever you go; in the grocery store, while in your vehicle, anywhere, and continue to be aware of it. Especially if you are worried, or in fear, breathe in this light. In fact, make it a habit to breathe light into your lungs as many times as you can.

If you sincerely take the time to do this meditation, you will notice the grand creation of magic and miracles in your life. Blessings!

∞

Eileen Siegel Bowen

4 GRATITUDE

"All moments are beautiful; only you have to be receptive and surrendering. All moments are blessings; only you have to be capable of seeing. All moments are benedictions. If you accept with a deep gratitude, nothing ever goes wrong.

A real prayer has nothing to suggest to God except a deep gratitude, thankfulness. It simply accepts whatsoever God is pouring. Prayer is receiving the gift." ~Osho

"As we express our gratitude, we must never forget that the highest appreciation is not to utter words, but to live by them."
~John F. Kennedy

∞

ALLOW FOR GRATITUDE TO HAPPEN

In moving from the mind, living in Trust, and surrendering to Divine will, gratitude happens.

Gratitude is not a concept of the mind. Gratitude arises only from quiet contemplation and observation. Gratitude arises when we move into the space of becoming the observer, noticing every moment of existence, noticing the grace and favor bestowed upon us, noticing the eternal goodness of life, and moving into the space of joy, love and excitement.

True Gratitude cannot be toward anything as gratitude happens for the All. When we live from the place of immense trust and surrender, every single aspect of life becomes sacred, the breath becomes holy, the body becomes holy, the ground we walk on becomes holy, every created being becomes holy, and every encounter with life becomes a sacred encounter. I am reminded of the words of Thich Nhat Hanh:

"Walk as if you are kissing the earth with your feet."

Nature and all of creation have been created to serve us, the Creator is serving us in the most wonderful ways, and do we stop to appreciate the Creator? If only we took the time to truly stay and watch and listen, we would come to appreciate and thank the Creator for all of the kind service given to us. I have noticed that appreciation and gratitude are the greatest portals that take us closer to the heart of the Creator.

At one time during my meditative state I asked the Creator, "How may I serve you more," and I was stunned and shocked to receive this answer loud and clear:

"Please allow me to serve you."

My heart wept with the understanding of this powerful message. I understood that I had been keeping a distance from the Creator thinking that I was born to serve the Creator and that I was not worthy to come closer to the Creator. After I received the message, I understood that the Creator was waiting to serve me, to please me with all of the most beautiful things around me in my life, and to keep me in love, joy, and excitement. And here I was, more worried about my service to the Divine by diligently praying and meditating, taking life so seriously, and forgetting to laugh or to be in joy. I realized that the greatest gift I can give the Creator is my joy. The Creator has gifted us this body, mind, the entire planet, and all the beautiful creations on it for us to enjoy and appreciate. The best gift we can give to the Creator is not any physical thing; it is our Joy.

As human parents, when we see our children living happy lives, it gives us extreme satisfaction; it is the same with the Creator. When we live in gratitude, we see life as endless Joy, and joy is the greatest gift we can give to the Creator.

∞

LOOKING THROUGH THE EYES OF GRATITUDE

At one time, I became so attached to my mind and its fear stories that I could literally feel fear as a heavy physical thing from my throat to my belly controlling my every action. I continued to pray for help every night before going to sleep. I had a strange dream where I was a body without the head, and I was walking down the street. I saw my body without the head yet I was not in any pain, and I heard a voice telling me again and again to put on the head. I did not understand the dream at that time. The same dream came to me again the next day. I woke up and without opening my eyes, I prayed for the meaning.

"Put on the head of God," was the answer that came.

The realization was that I was living in so much fear because I was seeing the world through my mind. My soul was asking me to get out of my mind and its fear stories. My soul was asking me to look at the world through the eyes of the Creator – the Creator whose infinite love and wisdom has created nothing other than excellence and eternal goodness around me.

I understood that I was loved so greatly that I was given complete dignity and freewill to create the world around me through my point of view. The vibration of life around me aligned itself to my state of consciousness. This I realized, was the grandest gift that helped me to know myself. It helped me to seek for answers and greater solutions, and it helped me to expand my consciousness as an eternal being of immense potentials.

This experience taught me to rejoice every time my mind showed me something dark, heavy, or fearful, and I knew that it would motivate me to search for greater solutions. I believe that this is true for every human being. As long as I believed the negative concepts about a person or situation from my mind, such as my neighbor should not be so loud, or my child should obey me, or she should not be so unkind, or the weather should not be so hot or cold, I would make it true for me. I would then project it on to the world around me and continue to create it. The Universe around me is so benevolent that it constantly seeks to prove me right.

This powerful realization made me to choose what I want to believe about myself or anyone else. As a healer, I realized that I could only help others when I am able to align myself with the eyes of Gratitude. My thirst to help others was wonderful but I also realized that unless I learn to look at life from the place of gratitude and align myself with my joy, I would not be able to help myself or anyone else.

If in my consciousness I am holding on to the concepts of suffering, then I have no light to shine for others. If I continue to help people from this consciousness, I will be only giving my attention to their pain. Therefore, my mind would get busy focusing on their anguish and amplifying it.

You cannot be fully present for people if you are focusing on their pain. Anyone in pain needs to hold the hand of a person who is emotionally strong, happy, and capable to see the best in them and in that situation. Not someone who is projecting the pain thus becoming completely helpless themselves.

I remember one occasion when I had visited with the nuns at Mother Teresa's "Home for the dying destitute" in India. It so happened on this particular day that they had found a man left to die on the streets. They picked him up, brought him to their center, and proceeded to give him a warm sponge bath. One of the nuns was holding the man while the other was sponging and cleaning him. The man gave a sigh, just closed his eyes, and died in the arms of the nuns. At first they were shocked, but when they realized he had died, they laughed. I was puzzled and asked them about it. The reply they gave me was so profound that I carry it in my heart to this very day. They said that Mother Teresa had shared with them the meaning of their service to humanity. She had said that God comes to us in distressing disguise to trigger the generosity and kindness in our hearts. Generosity is a concept; but unless we do an act of generosity, we do not understand what it is. So these nuns understood that the dying man was a definite distressing disguise of God helping them to awaken the generosity and kindness within them. They rejoiced and were thankful for this expansion of consciousness!

When we understand that a benevolent Creator created the world lovingly for us, we understand our experiences of expanded consciousness. And when we understand our experiences, we understand the world and in that understanding, comes Peace.

∞

GRATITUDE IS THE WAY

We are timeless beings, the earth-life is an adventure, and the body-mind is a tool to experience this adventure. The mind's work is to protect the body the best way it can. It attaches and identifies with everything it comes in contact with. It is interesting to note that the mind reassures itself through identification, attachment, and control because it knows only to do just that.

Living from identification with the mind, we collect a lot of baggage. Baggage loaded with judgments about ourselves and the world outside. Life seems to become darker, heavier, and does not feel good. It is wise to give thanks and ask for guidance at these times. For every moment of discord is a beautiful moment of realization. We are born into discord, but we need not be bound by it.

Life is an awesome experience, and experiencing life through a physical body is extraordinary! We, every human, animal, plant, and mineral, began as a thought in the mind of the Creator. When we appeared in physical bodies, we were built-in with the ability to wake up and expand our consciousness through every experience. The Creator knows and honors this innate ability in us that helps us in our infinite expansion, and each experience of expansion is beautiful, awesome, powerful, and enlightening!

We are created with the ability to transform our lives at any given moment. Every challenge comes to us to help us realize that the beliefs we now have about ourselves are keeping us trapped. It is time for us to break out of the belief and to empower and create ourselves anew. With any given challenge, we have the freewill to either refuse the lesson, or to choose to accept the experience with gratitude and allow it to empower us. Life is so benevolent that even when we choose to refuse to learn, the same lesson will come back again in another new form until we choose to learn and empower ourselves. The Creator's intention is for us to evolve into our Grander Selves.

∞

POWER OF GRATITUDE

When we are in the place of Gratitude, our body, mind and soul go through a tremendous healing. We become empowered by Gratitude. Consciously holding the attitude of Gratitude is the grandest prayer. It magnifies good feelings and brings joyous things to us in lightning speed.

Three years ago we moved to the South of Texas. The land had been experiencing a bitter drought and it was a record break of more than a 100 degree temperatures for more than 70 days. We had moved from North Carolina with its green trees everywhere, and Texas was a tumble-weeded contrast. There was nothing green in Texas, and even the grass was brown due to drought. There were no flowers or butterflies either. I decided to rejoice and give thanks. *It is very important to give thanks when you meet challenges, for these are contrasts shown by life to trigger your desire of creating beauty, joy, harmony, abundance and peace.*

Every time I saw the dry grass and trees, I visualized lush green meadows and green leaved trees with beautiful flowers and butterflies. I was in the place of magic in my mind's eye, and I was feeling happy. I continued to practice this feeling every day, and the feeling was so powerful that I even clapped my hands in glee sometimes as my feeling and visualizations were so real for me. We came to drought ridden Texas in July of 2009, and the rains began in August. It also rained a lot that winter, and as the land became green, I continued giving thanks and rejoicing. In March of 2010, there came colorful wild flowers of every kind along the wayside, in the grasslands, and in the fields. My heart was filled with laughter every time I went out for a drive. My neighbors told me that they had not seen so many wild flowers such as this for more than 3 years because of the drought. The land bloomed, the rivers filled, and the birds sang songs of happiness and abundance.

Practicing the attitude of Gratitude from deep contemplation and realization from within, allows us look at life with a better vision. Miraculously, things do get better. Gratitude and appreciation toward oneself, creates strong self-respect, high self-esteem, good health, and balanced emotions. Gratitude toward a parent, spouse, or child creates a grand loving relationship. Gratitude toward a friend, creates a beautiful friendship. Gratitude in the work place, creates peace, harmony, and friendly relationships among co-workers. Gratitude toward the land, creates abundance for life. Gratitude toward the environment, reduces the extremes of temperatures and natural calamities. Gratitude for the past experiences, stops dramas in one's life and creates an atmosphere of completion and peace. With Gratitude toward the Creator, we open our wellspring of love and joy from within. We become unstoppable, energizing batteries of love, joy, and peace in our life and for the Planet.

All things created, seen or unseen, gravitate toward the Attitude of Gratitude; it is a Universal Law!

Acknowledging this Law we become the Grand Creators of our reality. When we choose to see every life experience (good or bad) from the place of Gratitude, our heart opens and our life becomes a prayer – a gratitude prayer that is held in awe by the body temple.

The very moment Gratitude enters, every aspect of life – physical, emotional, and mental – every aspect of living is completely HEALED!

GRATITUDE IS THE GREATEST OF ALL PRAYERS
AND ALL VIRTUES.

∞

Eileen Siegel Bowen
SPIRITUAL TOOLS

Blessed be… A Prayer of Gratitude and Blessings from Sheryl Christian.

Thank you for the Divinity within me.
Thank you for making All things possible through love.
Thank you for the gift of miracles and peace in my presence – in every moment and for being always with me.
Thank you for the light and for the love and for All That Is.
Let the infinite and benevolent wisdom of the Creator fill me.
May the planet and all beings be blessed.
May every being awaken to eternal love.
Thank you… Blessed be…

Gratitude Journal

"Acknowledging the good that you already have in your life is the foundation for all abundance." ~Eckhart Tolle

A Gratitude journal is the first tool to bring abundance into your reality. Every progress in your life depends on Practicing Gratitude. Journaling all of the things that you are thankful for in your life is a great key for transformation.

Select a special notebook for yourself and write on the front page - *MY GRATITUDE JOURNAL*. Keep it in a place where you can see it often – perhaps near your bed. You can cover the notebook with pretty paper, paste beautiful pictures on it, or anything that you would like your notebook to have. Remember, this is a powerful tool to transform your life.

Take the notebook each night before going to bed, and write down three things that you were grateful for that day. As you continue to do this sincerely every day, you will notice that some days your list goes beyond three things. You will fill the journal with all of your blessings, and you will find that you will not be the same person again. A grand inner shift in your reality will have occurred. You will start focusing more and more on the abundance in your life, and you shall come to notice life as contentment and joy.

By holding the consciousness of joy, you will be creating a grand new future and fulfilling all of your dreams. You will be a grand witness to all of the magic and miracles in your life.

Visualization

Follow the grounding and centering meditations of chapter two.

Once you have centered yourself in the center of your head, spend time to think about the wonderful things in your life. Get in touch with the feelings of gratefulness for these things from your inner being. Amplify the feeling, meditate upon it, and make it as real as possible so that your physical body recognizes the joy of this feeling.

Take time to get in touch with this wonderful feeling, and from this place of happiness and gratitude, ask the Creator for wonderful things for that day or for your life. Imagine the feelings you would have if these wonderful things happened, affirm it to be true for you, and be in the place of excited anticipation.

End your visualization with a strong positive affirmation:

"This, or something better, is now manifesting for me in completely harmonious ways. It brings the highest good for all concerned."

Now clear your mind completely of the meditation and go about your day. If doubts or negative thoughts arise, let them go and just allow them to pass. Repeat this meditation everyday as often as you can. You can do it for five minutes or for thirty minutes. Make it interesting and enjoyable for you.

Being grateful for what you have and getting in touch with feelings of gratitude, is the powerful key for manifesting miracles in your life. Gratitude is an affirmation of abundance and is therefore a great key to manifest abundance. Abundance or lack depends absolutely on our perception.

∞

Diana Beardsley

5 DESERVEDNESS

"The world as we know is ruled by fear, chaos, limitation and greed. But YOU are not of this world. You come from somewhere else. And to the extent to which you remember that, you are lifted above the effects of the world. In becoming free of its chains, you become one of its redeemers." ~Marianne Williamson

"You can search throughout the entire universe for someone who is more deserving of your love and affection than you are yourself, and that person is not to be found anywhere. You yourself, as much as anybody in the entire universe deserve your love and affection."
~The Buddha

∞

FEELING WORTHY

Gratitude makes Joy to flow from within. Joy is the place where you can truly create what you want in your life. Every thought that takes joy away from you is stress.

We are born into a collective consciousness of fear. This fear programs us to believe in lack, to believe that we are not good enough, that we are not lovable, and that we are not worthy. Every social system is based on this theme with laws, rules, dogmas, competitions, and comparisons. We are born into this fear but it is not necessary for us to be bound by it.

The fear is a fear only while you are seeking approval and appreciation from the world outside. When you realize that you can create your life the way you want to, you will not need to seek to prove yourself to anyone else. Your power lies in your joy and your excitement. Listen to your heart and notice the things that you are passionate about.

In finding your true passion, put yourself completely into it. You will be surprised to notice that life has been waiting for you to follow your passion. You will begin to meet people who are in your path of joy, and new doors will open for your life. You come to realize that you were born with powerful gifts, and the gifts in you stir up the joy within every time you come in contact with anything related to your passion. Humans have been born with infinite gifts to empower themselves and to create grandness on this Planet. A wise human chooses to follow where joy and excitement lead knowing that the Universe is programmed to match our deepest desires and feelings.

There are no accidents, and there are absolutely no coincidences in life as we are the creators of our reality. Since the Universe is built to match our deepest feelings, what we feel about life is what we continue to create.

In the words of the Buddha:

"We are what we think. All that we are arises with our thoughts; with our thoughts we make the world."

As this is so, then let us decide for ourselves what kind of world we would like to create. If we choose to create a world of peace, harmony and goodwill, then we should be mindful to deliberately hold the consciousness of deservedness.

∞

THE UNCONSCIOUSNESS OF FEELING UNWORTHY

There are no mistakes in nature. We, each and every one of us, are here on this planet right now because we were meant to be here; it is a grand

Divine dispensation. We are a vital part of existence, and existence is not complete without us. If we were to look at existence as a huge jigsaw puzzle, each one of us are a piece of the puzzle, and the puzzle cannot be complete even if just one of us is not there.

The greater purpose of existence is to live life consciously every moment, and to transform the impossible into the possible through consciousness. This world is a classroom where we use the limited body to create unlimited experience of ourselves. You come to know the grandness of who you are by first experiencing who you are not. The classroom of the world is a launching pad from which you bounce yourself off to grander visions and greater experiences. This is an inner knowing and it is true for every human being.

When we resist or contradict this inner knowing, or we become lazy in consciousness, we continue to live from fear beliefs.

The feelings of unworthiness, lack of self-esteem and self-love, are all arrogance against creation. It is like throwing the gift of existence away. It is like pointing a finger at the Creator and saying that the Creator did not do the job perfectly in creating you. The Creator would never create something unworthy in the first place.

Seeking approval, seeking appreciation, comparing yourself, and competing with things on the outside arise from not loving yourself. The world around you is not in alignment with the source of Joy or God within. People around you do not appreciate what you like or do. They want you to please them and to not please your guidance from your inner being.

Aligning with the source of your Joy from your inner being, you remove stress from your life. Stop beating yourself up, stop pleasing others, go with your guidance, follow your feelings, and know that you deserve all good. Guilt, shame, disappointment, and depression come through comparison and competition stories of the mind. This keeps you down because it is not who you are. Every time you feel down, it is a clear indication for you to align back with your joy.

Aligning back with your joy helps you to manifest your desires effortlessly. You are like the ocean that contains all potentials, and your desires are the tiny waves that arise and fall. Do not think that you are only the wave as you are the mighty ocean with immense potentials to feel and create what you want in your life.

CREATING FROM THE PLACE OF DESERVEDNESS

"LIFE is a DREAM.
We are the dream makers.
Believe in the magic of dreaming.
Dreams don't just come true; they are already true.
Believe in your dreams and dare to dream.
There is a place of true magic inside you, take time to dream big.
Dream magical beautiful dreams." ~Premlatha Rajkumar

At one time there were about seven people connecting with me to help them manifest good jobs. They all had lost their current jobs and were in extreme stress. To help them, I decided to try the experiment myself. At that time I was a homemaker, living in a new country, did not know how to drive a car, did not have any contacts or know any local people, and literally did not know my way around.

I decided to connect with my desire for a job through my feelings of joy and deservedness. Every day, I imagined myself in a beautiful job, meeting people, and being in my passion. I worked up a happy feeling about it, and gave thanks for I knew that the Universe is more than willing to co-create with my feelings. I received so much joy and satisfaction from this visualization. Whenever I thought about the job market, or the rate of unemployment, I gently reminded myself that I was not in that rat race, that I was the creator of my reality. I continued to enjoy my imaginings and felt happy about it.

It so happened that I met a casual acquaintance in a group whom I did not know much about. I was prompted to talk to him, and I suddenly blurted out about my seeking for a job. I did not realize what I had done till he suggested that I send in my resume. I found out that he was a Human Resource Officer. He helped me to get a good job, a job that required team work, meeting new people, and so much more! I also found a neighbor who offered to carpool with me to work. It just so happened that he worked the same timings and that his office was just about 3 miles away from where I worked. Everything fell into place magically.

I shared this experience with these seven people who were searching for a job, and within the next month, all of them created wonderful jobs for themselves. Except for one person, all the others found jobs that paid them more than their previous jobs. This is the deservedness of our being! We are so greatly loved! When we choose to dream from the place of *worthy* and *happy*, we create our grandest realities.

Take time to create a sacred space for yourself and note down all of the grand creations that have already taken place in your life. Notice that they always started with your joyous desires and ended up as strong feelings in your heart. Think about how much you had desired certain things in your life, felt happy dreaming about them, and life brought you to situations that helped you to create them. It could have been a job you wanted, it could have been a place you wanted to go, or a particular clothing you wanted to wear. It can be any number of things; so just take time to note these things that you have already created in your reality. It reveals your capability to create effortlessly from the place of your joy. You cannot create things from your mind, only desires come from your mind, but feelings from the heart connect you to joy.

There are absolutely no limits in this Universe. It gives to you what you ask, but you must be in the place of trusting that you deserve it. And the moment you trust, you get out of the place of working hard for it or worrying or doubting. Just go be in the place of what brings you joy, excitement, and relaxation. Love yourself and give to yourself all that you feel would bring joy; take a walk, get a massage, fly a kite, blow bubbles, sit and dream, or do whatever you can do that would help you to raise your level of joy. This is the way of complete trust; your goodness comes to you in lightning speed. Being in the feeling of joy, happiness, and excitement is always the key.

∞

DO OTHER'S OPINIONS MATTER?

Seek approval from your inner being rather than from other people. Dwelling on others' opinions about you is a waste of time, and it is not your business in the first place. It is not going to help you in anyway.

People need not be your source of approval. You are the best person who can approve of yourself. Approve of yourself before anyone else can approve of you for the good job you have done, for the love that you are, for your kind heart, for all of the things you do, and for existing on this planet at this time. You are a grand being, and you are a very important part of the planet. By appreciating and approving of yourself, you will no longer seek approval on the outside, and you will not be dependent or addicted to others' opinions in anyway. You will be your own powerful guiding light.

The problem with depending on other people's approval, is that you dance to their tunes which are never true for you. You become addicted to the outside report and push yourself into stress. What others think of you is certainly not your business; however, living your life from the place of joy within and awakening yourself into a responsible, capable, loving, harmonious, and happy human is absolutely your business.

Buddha's Story

Once the Buddha was giving a spiritual discourse and there was an angry man who wanted to take out his anger on Buddha. He got up and started scolding and uttering all sorts of ugly words to the Buddha. The Buddha stood silently, with a smile on his face. After being spent of his anger, the man came up to the Buddha and asked:

"Don't you feel angry, are you not ashamed that I spoke like this to you in front of all these people?"

The Buddha in all his wisdom replied:

"Young man, you have an apple in your hand, and you are offering it to me, but I did not take it, so tell me where is the apple now?"

The man said that the apple is still with him, so the Buddha replied:

"Likewise your words are with you, I did not make them mine."

Reminder: Do not make the opinions of others' as yours. Allow people to have their opinions, BUT DO NOT MAKE THEM YOURS.

Love, approve, and cherish yourself completely to remove yourself from getting addicted to people's approval. It is always stressful and difficult to compete with others, compare your situation, or belittle your actions by considering what you should or should not have done. Freedom is giving the gift of KINDNESS to oneself. It means never allowing fear, anger, or sadness to cloud your life. It means to live life with total acceptance, flexibility, and without resistance. There is no success to be achieved, and there is no failure either. For whatever you are doing at any given moment with total love and acceptance, is the Ultimate Success.

This Prayer of Byron Katie is a powerful reminder:

"God spare me from the desire for love, approval, or appreciation."

∞

YOU DESERVE THE BEST; ASK AND YOU WILL RECEIVE

The approval of the Divine Presence is around us always. The Divine communicates with us all of the time, but we have not trained our senses to listen and observe. The communication from the Divine is not like that of the human mind – it can be received only from the place of conscious noticing.

You can start noticing divine communication with physical evidence. Connect with your center, and silently ask for a sign of Divine communication. You can ask to see heart shapes, faces in the clouds, butterflies, feathers, pretty rocks, or anything that would signify a physical evidence for you. Now, let go the thought, be in the place of conscious noticing, and you will be surprised by the amazing ways of Divine communication. This brings you to the place of confidence, guidance, healing, and release of fear. You can use this method of communication in many creative ways throughout your life in different situations. Ask and you will receive answers. Do this and you will know that you are so greatly loved, you are never alone, and you are lovingly embraced and carried in the arms of the Divine. Be in the place of complete trust that you deserve whatever you are asking, and then ask.

Creating from your deservedness involves making your Spiritual Practice the center of your life. Simple spiritual practices for everyday are living in gratitude, surrounding yourself with positive people if you can, claiming your dreams, speaking confidently about yourself, learning to communicate in positive affirmative words, talk about what you love about you, seeking to enhance your joy by doing things that uplift you, meditating, and observing silence every day. Rising out of the fear consciousness of the Planet involves real spiritual work. Do the work on yourself, and be the magician of your life.

∞

THE MEANING OF ABUNDANCE

We emanated from the Creator. The Creator being is infinite positive creative energy that constantly seeks to expand and create itself anew every moment. We, as part of the Creator being, constantly create and expand ourselves every moment. Hence, the past does not have any power over us as every moment we are creating better solutions and creations for ourselves. Only the mind holds records of the past, and the opinions of the people in our life. But again, as these are only records, we also have the power to drop them and let them go.

This Planet of duality is a powerful place of creation, and we are born into duality to experience who we are not. And every experience of who we are not brings stress. From this place, we seek to desire the opposite, to expand, to create greater solutions, and to know who we are. We become who we are not – in order to know who we are. This is the great secret of existence on this Planet at this time. Life always moves forward; it does not recede backward.

It is your nature that whenever you see something limiting you, you search for a solution, and the search or the journey for the solution keeps you in the excitement. This is the power of the creative energy you are feeling. The moment the goal is achieved, your excitement is not there anymore, and so you search to see for more limitations and seek to create even grander solutions. The mind does not understand these things. The mind analyzes and attaches the excitement to the goal and continues to hoard the goal by thinking that was the joy or excitement. But the true excitement came when the job was being done, and when the journey was being made. There is nothing to achieve, but everything to experience. The energy involved in creating solutions is the most beautiful experience.

We continue to evolve and expand in infinite ways and discover our abundance.

Abundance has nothing to do with wealth, money, or results. Everything in this Planet has been created for us, every person, every situation, and every place is there for us to know ourselves from a grander perspective. There is never any possibility of failure. As Spirit beings, every experience of physicality is our grand success whether the mind accepts it or not. You can be as creative, good, talented, and adventurous as you like. You can give your energy fully and completely every moment toward the physical experience, and come into the realization that what you have is enough, and is more than enough. This is your abundance as you are the richest person on the Planet!

Giving attention and energy fully and completely every moment, the physical experience becomes a great joy. When I slow down to savor with complete reverence of the work I do with my physical body, I have noticed that every act becomes sacred and that every act is perfect. If I am washing the dishes, I am in the place of success; if I am cleaning an object, I am in the place of success; if I am feeding my body with my hand, I am in the place of success; if I am hugging my daughter, I am in the place of success. Everything I do in the physical with conscious connection, is my ultimate success. I have completely savored the moment, and I am living in abundance. True abundance is acknowledging the magnificence of our beingness.

∞

SPIRITUAL TOOLS

The Spiritual Practice from the place of deserving. "The Upanishads" are a collection of philosophical texts of ancient India. They are the collection of experiences of a 108 people who followed the path of self-realization. These people went into their heart, into their inner kingdom, and found that everything on the outside – the mountains, the sun, trees, people, and everything was a reflection of their inner world. They realized that everything on the outside begins from the inner kingdom. The main teachings of this philosophy are that *HUMANITY IS DIVINE* and that the purpose of Human life is to realize that *HUMAN NATURE IS DIVINE*.

You are a Divine being. The Universe matches the consciousness that you hold on the inside; there are absolutely no mistakes. You are the Creator of your Reality!

The most important thing is to love yourself enough to practice your tools. Get out of negative places and hang around positive people. Stop watching commercials, negative TV serials and news. Instead, connect with nature, take a walk, sit under a tree, read a book, observe your breath, draw, watch funny movies and videos, or do anything that you enjoy to raise the level of peace and happiness inside you.

Every day, sit in silence with yourself, center yourself, and use a notebook for your Spiritual Practice. In the notebook, list all of the things you love about yourself. Keep adding to the list every day. Notice that your joy and excitement rise as you continue to write and think about all of the things you love about yourself. Claim it every day. Give this precious gift to yourself.

The list can be made like this:
I love myself.
I love my physical body.
I love my courage.
I love my humor.
I love my sense of adventurousness.
I love my intuition.
I love the way I laugh.
I love the way I see things.
I love connecting with people.
I love the way I do my job.
I love to feel good.
I love my art.
I love to be around beautiful things.
I love my cooking.
I love what I write.
I love to work with my hands.
I love to plant new things.

Feed the list everyday with more and more things that you love about yourself. Your Spirit will shine and let the Universe know that you are ready to manifest more and more of all that you love. You are a divine, magnetic being and you will attract the situations and people that match your consciousness. You need not go in search as everything will come to you. Know that you are a beautiful creator and what you hold in your consciousness, you will create.

∞

A POWERFUL STORY TO SHARE
Meeting the Man of My Dreams

My parents had adopted me and I grew up as a lonely child. My experience with authority figures, especially the male energy, was terrorizing and very early in life I decided that I will have nothing to do with a man in my life; I dreamed of a contented life living alone.

I was doing my Masters in Human Development, and I had to prepare for a seminar on marriage and family. I brought home a pile of books from the library to prepare for my seminar. I do not remember the name of this particular book; all I remember is this particular sentence in this book that changed my life magically. The book was explaining about marriage for youngsters who were in search of life partners. It said:

"The person who will be your life partner, exactly the way you would like him/her to be, is already born and living somewhere on the Planet; so prayerfully intend for this person to appear in your life at the right time, and ask the Creator to bless this person every day."

I was amazed by this sentence, my curiosity got the better of me, and I decided to experiment and see for myself if such a person with all the personalities I like exists anywhere on this Planet. So from the place of deservedness, gratitude, and joy, I visualized this nameless, faceless person of my dreams everyday by doing the *MIRACLE LIGHT PRAYER* and enjoyed the feeling of finding this person, and noticing that this person is so wise, kind, romantic, and loving.

After about a month of doing this visualization, I was very familiar with this energy of the nameless, faceless person. I felt so happy whenever I thought about him. It was my secret and no one knew about it.

I was at a shopping center with my parents one day, my parents had met a coworker of theirs from their office, and they started chatting about their work. I was so bored and as I could not join in their conversation, I just watched them. Suddenly a feeling crept into me, and I recognized it as my secret happy feeling about this nameless, faceless person.

I turned around and I saw this tall handsome boy behind me. He was looking at me, and I looked into his eyes and could not take my eyes off him. I knew the feeling, and I understood that this was the nameless, faceless, person of my visualization. I was shocked and excited at the same time! I also recognized him as John, the son of one of my father's friends. I did not know him well though I had seen him once a long time ago in a wedding. He knew my father, saw him at the shopping place, and had come to greet him.

My heart leapt for joy, and I knew that I had to let my joy happen.

Growing up in India, there were limitations. I could not tell my parents about this because in India, parents searched for a groom for their daughters and not the other way around.

I had an idea. I knew John's father, and he was a very kind man, so I met John's father and told him about my decision. I told him that this was a very powerful guidance for me from Spirit, and I requested of him to speak to my parents and also to his son about this.

He was amazed by my request, but he did speak to my parents and we were married!

Later, my husband John told me that on the day we met at that shopping mall, something had made him to get down from his bus two stations before his station and walk in to the mall where he saw my father. He said that when I turned and looked at him, he felt a magical energy pass through him.

It is now twenty-five years since we got married, we are like any ordinary married couple, we do have our arguments, yet we keep our magic alive. Every day, we find things to appreciate about each other; we talk to our children and our friends about how we met each other. We celebrate and claim our love every day. We continue to feed our love with all of the things that make us feel romantic and joyful. Hence, even today when I get a glimpse of my husband back home from his office and parking his car, my heart skips a beat.

I have shared this story with my children, my students, many of my friends, and many youngsters. I have also witnessed the magic many have created from this sharing. I see that it has helped them to choose their life partners by raising their consciousness of joy from the place of gratitude and deservedness. Manifesting from the place of joy, keeps one in wellbeing and true deservedness.

∞

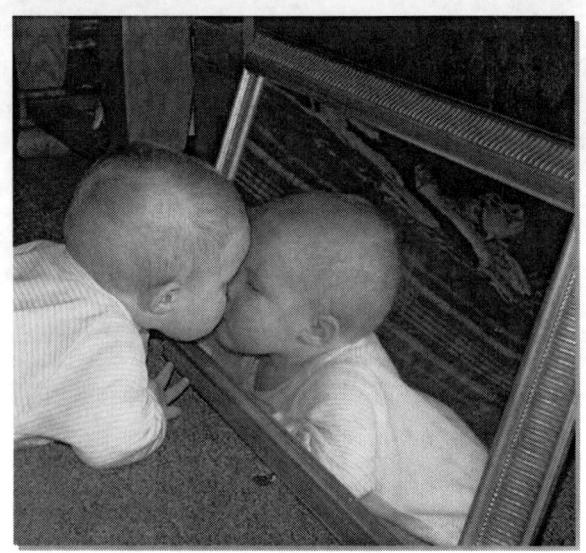

"Beauty is eternity gazing at itself in a mirror.
But you are the eternity and you are the mirror."
~ Khalil Gibran, *The Prophet*

6 LOVING THE SELF

"Love knows no bodies, and reaches to everything created like itself. Its total lack of limit is its meaning. It is completely impartial in its giving, encompassing only to preserve and keep complete what it would give." ~*A Course in Miracles*

"The heart is like a flower – unless it is open it cannot release its fragrance into the world. The fragrance of the heart is made up of the qualities and virtues of our spirit. Most of us have learned how to keep our heart closed in a world that would trample all over us if we let it. Being open hearted today seems to require tremendous courage. A closed heart is in need of opening. And when you do, you will have begun to heal yourself." ~ Osho

"Appreciation and self-love are the most important tools that you could ever nurture. Appreciation of others, and the appreciation of yourself is the closest vibrational match to your Source Energy of anything that we've ever witnessed anywhere in the Universe." ~Abraham

∞

TRUE LOVE AND EGO LOVE

This chapter on "loving the self" cannot be explained from just the form or the physical aspect of oneself, it needs to be explained from both the form and the formless selves of a person. For that which we call as love from the physical, is an emotion that arises from attachment to mind stories and opinions about persons and things. True love is a state of being, and a conscious state of connection with all beings. It is the state that gives rise to trust, surrender, gratitude, and compassion.

When one is not aware of oneself beyond the physical, true love cannot happen as there would only be the ego love for the self. Ego love does not bring happiness, it brings misery, for it always attaches to mind stories of possessing, comparing, and competing. The ego tries to mould the other in its ideas and opinions, and when the other is not in tune with its ideas or opinions, then it becomes miserable. In ego love, there is always a division of oneself and the other, there is always an otherness of the other, and the ego love tries to destroy all otherness. The ego love is not true love because it is just a love for the reflection and not the true being. All that which is physical, is an image and a reflection of the true being.

From knowing the true self, which is both the form and the formless, one comes into understanding, clarity, and peace. Loving becomes your nature and you become love. When you become *LOVE*, you cannot love a particular thing as your love is a sacred state of connection with the *ALL*.

∞

UNCONDITIONAL LOVE – TRUE LOVE

Everything in nature vibrates with love. Animals teach us true love without conditions; if we stand under a tree, it fully gives its shade, its fruits, and it gives everything of itself to us unconditionally without expecting anything in return. It neither has likes nor dislikes. Nature is the best teacher of unconditional love. Unconditional Love – True Love has no expectation.

Unconditional love can never happen in the mind; the mind is full of needs and opinions, and the love of the mind is always a bargain.

"If you are good to me, I am good to you, and then I love you," this is the love of the mind.

True love is unconditional, it is giving the gift of freedom to the other, and it is the state of grace that transforms the sickness of divisions, hate, and misery.

Emotional love or ego love can understand only *me and the other*, but true love understands *me and the other me*. True Love cannot divide as it knows that it is the All. Ancient traditions of indigenous peoples point out to the Greatest truth that:

> "I am the other. Without the other, I would not exist. If there is no one to call me by my name, or talk to me, or acknowledge my presence, then I DO NOT EXIST!"

The ancient Mayan tradition of greeting people "In Lak'ech Ala k'in," which means, "I am you and you are me," is a wonderful way to remind oneself that "I do not exist without other people in my life."

When we open our hearts to true love, we cannot love any one person or any one particular thing, we can only be the love that we are. When one is full of love, there is no need for something on the outside to create love. Moving away from true love, is always a struggle.

Practicing silence, taking time to witness life, and choosing to accept reality, makes us more loving; not toward a particular person, but we become the wellspring of unconditional love. Then nothing in life can disappoint us, for life becomes an adventure to discover. Unconditional LOVE is who we are.

∞

THE FUNDAMENTAL REASON TO LOVE ONESELF

Creation happens through holding and focusing consciousness. The spiritual truth – "as above so below, as within, so without" – is the code of creation on this Planet. To avoid chaos and confusion, it is very important to focus and hold the right consciousness within oneself.

If we are not aware of our multidimensional expressions, and our true connection to Source-God, we will not love ourselves, and we will allow others to manipulate and control us. Knowing our true selves and how creation works, we fulfill our real purpose in being in a human body at this time.

Life experience on this Planet is duality, the experience of both the light and the dark has been the norm for eons. The mind is constantly labeling some as light and some as dark by the way it perceives things. The mind always leads one to confusion. Confusion leads to condemning situations and people. Condemning is dangerous because when we condemn something and try to repress it, it creates the opposite effect. For that which you repress, struggles to be expressed. Therefore, even if we struggle with it and not allow it, it will express itself in a different form. And the more we focus on the things that we perceive from the mind as wrong, the more we will create it, for focusing on a particular consciousness within, creates it without.

Love begins from the self, and if we do not know how to love ourselves, we cannot love anyone else. If we continue to judge and condemn ourselves and feel that we are worthless, then we will do the same to the person living next to us and the world at large. The most dangerous person on the Planet, is the one who cannot love himself. This person will be an angry person who would not hesitate to destroy himself, other humans, or the Planet in the name of religion, patriotism, or borders that can be noticed only on a map. For many years, religions and society have kept us within the walls of self condemnation. This is the reason for all of the wars from ancient days till today.

When we condemn ourselves, love becomes impossible. We cannot love ourselves, we cannot love others, we will not allow others to love us, and neither will we allow God to love us. Fear and guilt are the most debilitating feelings in a person and can allow this person to be easily exploited as they will not fight back nor be rebellious.

We accepted the Creator's offer and chose to come into these physical bodies at this time. Each one of us is a unique creation of the Creator. There is an amazing amount of love and wisdom poured into the creation of a human being. This Planet runs on duality as duality is an exciting opportunity to take advantage and grow from. Every contrasting situation in life, is an opportunity to create a grander solution and harvest wisdom. This is the most exciting purpose of life. We are born with immense power to overcome obstacles and create grander and greater beauty on the Planet. Our power comes from our union with our Divine Presence and not from our mind.

Human life becomes meaningful if it is lived from the place of divine union with our soul's purpose. Moving beyond the mind and its fear concepts, and accepting and loving oneself completely, helps one to move forward in life with ease and grace. A person who loves and accepts himself, is willing to explore and awaken the wisdom within himself and the Universe. This person is capable of creating "Heaven" on Earth.

∞

CONNECTING WITH THE HEART

The Planet is awakening into its Grand light of Oneness, and you as a Divine being were sent here to the Planet at the right time.

Working our Divinity in physicality is what we came here to do. Forgetting our Divinity is the greatest illusion on this Planet. In the eyes of God, everyone is pure, holy, blameless, and childlike. Remembering that each of us is pure and holy, we acknowledge our Divinity and help others to remember theirs by seeing them with the eyes of God.

In India "Namaste" is a wonderful way of greeting others. This word is a sacred Sanskrit word that has a deep meaning. Namaste is a salutation done when people meet each other. In South India, the word is said as "Namaskaram." The deeper meaning of this beautiful word is powerfully awakening human consciousness.

Namaste or Namaskaram means, "I acknowledge that my body is the temple where the Divine resides, and I also acknowledge that your body is a temple for the Divine, and so the Divine in me salutes the Divine in you."

Namaste or Namaskaram is said by looking into the eyes of the person in front of you, folding your palms in front of your heart, and gently bowing your head. In this way, you salute the Divine.

This is a powerful way of reminding one another to love God in the other person.

The extent to which you can love another human being absolutely depends on the extent to which you are connected with respect and gratitude to your own Divine Essence.

Every ancient tradition urges one to connect and live in love from the heart. The modern world and its busyness have taken people away from their hearts and have kept them in their mind; there is no room for the heart or for true love. This was the fall of consciousness. The chaos and confusion created by the busyness of the present world, has removed peace and harmony from people's lives. It is imperative that we connect back to the heart, to true love, and to our Divine Presence within.

The heart is our sacred sanctuary; it is the place where we are one with our Divinity. Connecting with the heart helps us to understand the truth of who we are. Our heart is aligned with the love and light of our Celestial soul. When we live from our heart, we are in the place of our power, and we will be given immense protection and guidance.

When we connect with our heart from the center of our head, we understand the complete union with our Source-Creator and with all life. Knowing ourselves as directly emanating from Source, we need not give away our power to anyone, nor do we need to take power over others. We come to understand divine equality of all beings and we become responsible creators of our reality.

∞

EMPOWERMENT

Thoughts, feelings, words, and ideas are constantly attracting their likeness from the Universe. When we focus our thoughts clearly, we produce effective and desirable results. This is a most important knowing that has been lost and hidden for many years, and for many years people have been continuously creating their experiences by default.

We create our reality and that is the TRUTH. Reality begins as a thought or a feeling and then manifests in the physical.

Our collective denial of our power has created much chaos and confusion. To break free from this trance, we must come back to our own worthiness and be willing to feel genuine love and appreciation for who we are. Loving the Self as a part of the Creator energy of wisdom and power, is the essential key to attract the very best experiences that life has to offer.

When we feel genuine love for the Self, we are connecting with the vital force that sustains all of existence; therefore, it is the greatest gift we offer to the Planet.

One of the powerful ways to create this loving relationship with the Self is the mirror exercise. Stand in front of a mirror for five to ten minutes in the morning and in the evening and gaze into the eyes of the person in the mirror. Open your heart and say the words aloud "I love you."

At first this may sound silly, for you are not used to loving yourself, but if you continue to participate in this exercise consistently, you will find that you come into your personal power. You will find that you have stopped seeking love from others, for you have given much love to you, and you become a wellspring of love to others.

The love we create will support, guide, and inspire us in every aspect of life. We will be inspired to make wise and powerful choices for ourselves.

Loving the Self is now our assignment on this Planet. We then need not search for ourselves in others. When we start loving who we are, then we do not need anyone to make us a someone.

Loving and accepting the Self, brings contentment and joy. You become your own best friend. You start living in your Truth. You do not seek to compete or compare yourself with others anymore, self-confidence radiates from you, and you see yourself as a success every moment. This is the greatest empowerment!

Choose to love and celebrate YOU! You are a magnificent creation. One of a kind; there was no one born like you nor will there ever be one born like you as nature never repeats itself! Celebrate YOU! You deserve the Best!

Affirmations on loving the Self are very empowering. Affirmations work wonders on everyone who chooses to empower themselves sincerely.

You can do affirmations like these everyday to empower yourself:

I love myself.
I am wonderful.
I am a beloved child of the Universe, the Creator, of God.
I deserve to live a wonderful life.
All is well in my world.
I am beautiful!

This world is the reflection of my thoughts, my gratitude, and my light. I consider myself to be beautiful, and I create a world of beauty with beautiful people!

Affirmations receive their magic from the feelings you bind with the words. Pour your feelings on to every word of the affirmation you say and make them true for yourself. You can do these affirmations by looking at yourself in the mirror, or you can write them many times during the day as a love letter to the Self, or you can recite them with feeling many times during the day. Whatever you choose to do sincerely, will work for you. This is a great way to remove the drama from your life.

When you awaken to your personal power, you will find that you create more peace, harmony, and freedom in your life. People who are able to live in loving kindness within their own selves, are the greatest gifts to this Planet.

If you are choosing to love yourself, then discovering the unity with your Spirit and your Celestial Soul is an essential part of your journey into self-discovery and awakening to your Divine Presence.

∞

A POWERFUL SPIRITUAL TOOL TO ANCHOR UNCONDITIONAL LOVE AND ACCELERATE OUR SPIRITUAL EVOLUTION

PRANIC BREATHING – BREATHING GOD

Prana is a Sanskrit word for *LIFE*. Prana means the *breath of God*. Prana is consciousness; it is the life force energy of the Planet. It is also called by many names around the world as "Ki" energy, "Chi" energy, "tachyon" energy, or "orgone" energy. It is the energy stream of wellbeing – it is the light particle that creates life and sustains life.

In the ancient days, many practiced pranic breathing and lived longer lives filled with wellbeing. Even today, those who practice pranic breath are able to live a life of wellbeing and peace even in the midst of chaos. This life force energy comes from the Sun, and the Sun receives it from beyond our solar system. All live foods obtained from plants; like fresh fruits, vegetables, and nuts are full of prana energy, and they give immediate health and energy for the body. As we started cooking food and eating dead food, like animal products, we deprived our bodies of vital life force energy. The body suffered manifesting disease and discomfort. Believing fear concepts of the mind also blocks this life force energy from entering into our body.

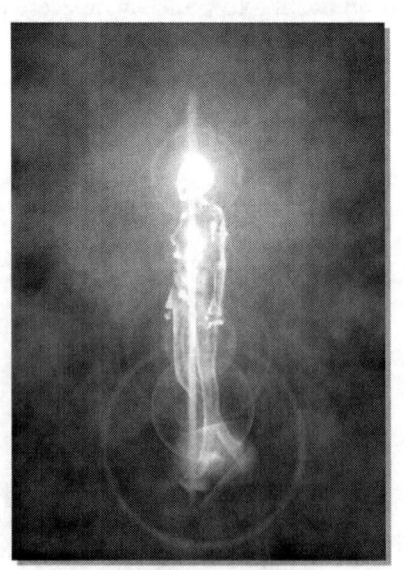

The Pranic Tube

Pranic breathing is not done through the lungs, it is done through the prana tube thorough visualization. The diameter of the prana tube is roughly 2 inches. The prana tube extends directly through the center of your body. It runs through the pineal gland, extends above the head, runs down through the perineum, and extends below your feet. The heart is in the center of the prana tube. We are multidimensional beings as we are not only the physical form, but also we exist as the formless soul and spirit. Pranic breathing is done from the physical form by giving attention to the formless in us. Our body of form exists by the greater assistance of our spirit and our soul, which are formless. Spiritual scientists who practiced alchemy noticed that at the time of death, consciousness separated into two separate entities called the "BA" and the "KA" bodies.

The "BA" Body

The "BA" is immortal and it is the Celestial Soul. It is outside space and time. It is a blinding, brilliant, liquid light about arm's distance above your head. You can connect and communicate with the "BA" body only by appreciation and gratitude from the heart. The "BA" body is connected directly to the heart. Hence, connecting from the feeling of appreciation and gratitude, we can connect to the "BA" body – our Celestial Soul.

The "BA" body brings immense protection and healing to the physical body. The *"Miracle Light Prayer"* in the chapter on Surrender is the mode of connection with the BA body or your Celestial Soul. It is described in all spiritual literatures as the spark of Divinity that resides within us. It is the aspect of our multidimensional selves that inspires us to move beyond our ego and animal nature and experience the interconnectedness of all life.

In many spiritual traditions, the BA is referred as the Great I AM Presence, which is a mighty individualized presence of God. This individual Presence is a mighty part of you – it is a glorious creative being, full of love, joy, and boundless optimism for your future together. When a person lives in close communion with his I AM Presence, his physical body transforms to youth, beauty, and wisdom.

The physical body was created to live in close union with the Celestial Soul and Spirit; however, the fall of consciousness led to the loss of this knowledge, and the incorrect use of our creative energy has made the physical body to experience disease and death.

In sacred Egyptian hieroglyphs, the BA body is written as a winged human head or sometimes as a human faced bird.

The "KA" Body

The "KA" body is our energy body. It is the spirit or etheric twin of our physical body; it is invisible and is in the same shape and size as our physical body. It envelops and interpenetrates the physical body. The "KA" body or the spirit is focused in the pineal gland in the center of the head. The *"center of the head"* meditation in chapter 2 (Belief and Trust) is a powerful meditation that connects you with your spirit body.

The "KA" is the pranic body and it contains the pranic tube. Our KA body is directly connected to the highly benevolent Spiritual Realms. By our intention and focus on our KA body, we can draw benevolent spiritual energies that heal our physical body and also help us to accelerate our spiritual evolution.

But by our unconsciousness and attachment to our mind stories of fear, we have fragmented our KA bodies and have a very low spiritual energy. Our KA bodies are deeply connected to the experiences of our physical form. Every time we go into fear, we fragment our KA body. Every emotional desire and attachment from the mind for a person or an object makes our KA body to break into pieces and these pieces attach to the things of our desire.

It is a practice in the country side of India that when a dying person is not able to let go the spirit, they find out what deeper desire and attachment is not allowing the spirit to move on. If the person had an attachment to money, they would take a coin and put it in water and feed that water to the dying man. If the attachment was to the fields or the land, then they brought a piece of rock or dirt from the land and put that in a glass of water and fed the dying person. Amazingly, within just a few spoonfuls, the dying person easily let go of their spirit.

In ancient Egypt, people lived conscious lives, they possessed the minimum objects, and also buried their possessions with them when they died. They understood this concept of attachment to things; for wherever we put out strong desires, our KA breaks apart and a piece of it attaches to the object of our desire. Also, the objects we possess in life hold a part of our KA energy. That is why psychics can hold an object used by a person and perceive their life story. When we collect back our fragmented KA body, we are in our spiritual power and we can manifest peace and harmony in our lives.

Ancient Egyptians and ancient people of the East believed that existence is eternal and continues after the death of the physical body, and that whatever happened in the physical would also mirror in the afterlife. Hence, they were very careful about their interactions with people, whether it be business, sex, friendship, or any relationship. They chose to avoid negative experiences and live with integrity by developing their higher spiritual attributes of truth, clarity, compassion, and wisdom.

Bridging the Mind and the Heart

Our physical heart is directly connected to our BA body or our Celestial Soul. All abundance, healing, and protection come from our Celestial Soul, which is also called our great I AM Presence.

Our KA body or Spirit Body resides in the center of our head in the pineal gland.

When we connect with our Spirit and move into the sacred space of our hearts, we create the golden bridge between the heart and the mind, and we enter into the Union or Oneness of our True Selves. When we are in this oneness, we become the wellspring of wisdom and unconditional love.

Connecting with the Heart

Create a sacred space, ground yourself, and center yourself in your head. Notice your breathing. Feel yourself in the center of your head. You have now connected with your Spirit – your Spirit works with you through your intention.

As mentioned earlier, due to the fall in consciousness we have fragmented our Spirit body by living from the mind. It is very important now to bring back your Spirit from wherever you have left it.

The exercises for forgiveness in the 1st Chapter are powerful to bring back your Spirit. Only when your Spirit is wholesome, can you have access to the benevolent Higher Spiritual Realms.

Another powerful method of calling back your Spirit to you is by using the Rose Tool.

The Rose Tool

Practice the Rose tool often to replenish your energy-KA-body-spirit body, and be in the place of your power.

Your ability to imagine and visualize from the center of your head is your greatest tool. Imagination and visualization is energy work. When you are able to be in a quiet, undisturbed space, have centered, and think of it in your Spirit-Presence, then it already is. Being present with yourself, you are always in control. Energy work takes practice, but there is no right or wrong way to do energy work. When you are sincere and consistent in your practice, you will attain success.

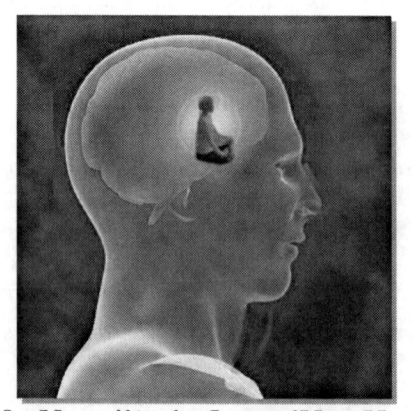

See Yourself in the Center of Your Head

You could be sitting comfortably in a chair and looking at the world through your eyes as windows. Now put out your right hand in front of you. The space where your fingers touch is the space where you can place your blank view screen. Now close your eyes, look at your view screen, and know that it is there. Practice looking at the screen and also noticing your breath at the same time. Noticing your breath keeps you away from thoughts. Imagine a rose on your view screen; make it as real as possible.

My teacher, Jim Self, gave a wonderful explanation of why we use the rose as a tool. He said that every plant on the planet has a particular vibrational frequency that is measured in Hertz. All plants, herbs, and trees range from 0-210 cycle/sec Hertz of frequency. Sandalwood and frankincense have the highest of 210 Hertz. But amazingly, the Belgian red rose has a frequency of 800 hertz which is way higher than any other of the plant species.

Also from my personal experience, I have noticed that the arrangement of petals in a Rose flower is a form of sacred geometry, which is the feminine energy pattern of the Creator. I see artists who paint pictures of deities like Mother Mary, Mary Magdalene, Lady Nada, paint the picture of a red rose in the place of their heart. From my experience with the rose tool, I know that every time we use the ROSE as a tool, it steps up our vibrational frequency and aligns us with our powerful creative energies.

From the center of your head, see your view screen with a red rose. See the rose as very real with soft petals, dewdrops on it, see a stem, a few leaves, and make it as natural as you have seen it in nature. Now explode the rose, and see it dissolve into zillions of tiny light particles. Practice this for fun.

Now when you feel confident of practicing this you can create a rose in your view screen and ask the rose silently or aloud:

"Let all the energy of my Spirit that I have given away or left behind return to me now."

Wait and notice the feeling, the sensations, and even images of people or places where you have lost your energy will appear at this time. Notice that your rose has changed color or it has become bigger. When you feel complete, allow the rose to explode into a zillion tiny light particles; just allow them to dissolve.

People place their attention on you every day, they want things from you or they want thing to be done by you. It can be your spouse, children, coworker, or even a stranger. It is important that we give people's energy that are in our space back to them.

Create another rose in your view screen and ask this rose to remove the energies of people who have left them in your space and to give it back to them. Wait and feel the sensations and watch the images that come up. Understand that the energies of other people are being removed and given back to them. Notice the rose change color or become bigger. Allow the rose to explode into light particles and dissolve.

This is a powerful gift you can give to people so that they will also be able to complete themselves and be in their power. And you get back your Spirit energy to be in the place of your power.

Now invite the brilliant light of your Celestial Soul to fill the gaps that were left by the removal of other people's energies.

Breathe in and feel the love and light filling every part of you and making you your wholesome self.

Moving into the Physical Heart

Take a day or two to practice being in the heart while noticing the heart beat.

From the center of your head become aware of your physical heart. You can place the palm of your hand on your heart, take a breath, and bring your consciousness to the pressure of feeling your hand on your chest. Take a deep breath in through the nose and out through the mouth. This kind of breath brings clarity and ease.

Practice feeling your heart, concentrating on your breath, and send thoughts of love to your heart. Your heart is a being of love, and it responds to your love and appreciation. Bringing your attention to your heart is so powerful that you will experience peace and calm, and even sometimes unexpected solutions will arise for a present problem. By connecting to your heart, you are connecting to your wellspring of wisdom and abundance in all aspects of your life. Practice being with your heart and feeling your heart. In times of fear or worry, place your hand on your heart and breathe in lungfulls of light; it is a powerful help.

After you have practiced grounding, being in the center of your head, calling your Spirit back with the help of the rose tool, and being in the Presence of your heart, it is time to activate your pranic tube.

Activating the Prana Tube

Your Spirit-KA body is the source of life force energy for your physical body; the physical body is alive because of the KA body. As the KA body is connected to the higher spiritual realms, developing your KA body will give you an extraordinary advance into higher consciousness.

The awakening process for every human on the planet at this time involves life force energy. Your KA body receives the life force energy from Source-God. Breathing the life force energy, you are breathing God.

The goal of Pranic Breathing is feeling connection with all life through conscious breathing. Conscious breathing is breathing with God. Whatever you choose to put inside your physical body, such as the kind of foods, drinks, thoughts, perceptions, and emotions, all help either to build or to diminish your KA or spirit body. The choice is always yours.

Pranic breathing keeps you centered in your heart and your pineal gland that are in connection to your Celestial Soul and your Spirit. Breathing prana energy will keep you grounded and securely connected to the cosmos and the earth. You will be mentally and emotionally balanced, and you will not be affected by the negative energies of people.

Go within, be in the center of your head, observe your breathing, and say silently or aloud, "I activate my prana tube now."

Visualize and feel your crystalline prana tube; it is about 2 inches in diameter. It extends right through the center of your body. Further extending up through your pineal gland in your brain, moving on to connect with your cosmic chakras (above your aura above your head), and it extends down through your perineum just above your anus thus moving down below your feet and into the earth.

Begin to inhale prana energy through your physical breath by visualizing your breath moving in up from the earth through your prana tube to your heart chakra, and feel the life force of the planet flowing through you and expanding your heart. Be in the place of Gratitude and Appreciation for this gift, send love from your heart to Mother Earth, and continue to do this breathing till the Earth responds by sending her love back to you (you will receive this message as a feeling in your heart).

Now begin to inhale prana through your physical breath by visualizing your breath moving in from the cosmic above your head, down to your crown center, into your pineal gland, and feel it activated. Feel this prana move down to your heart center. Feel this cosmic energy expand and move you in a most profound way thus allowing you to remember your spiritual essence. Be in the place of Gratitude and Appreciation for this gift, send love from your heart to Father Sky, continue to do this breathing, and wait till the cosmos responds by sending his love back to you (you will receive this message as a feeling in your heart). You are now acknowledging and accepting your connection as the Divine Child of Father-Mother God.

With the next in-breath, breathe prana energy from above and below at the same time, up through your perineum into the heart and down through your pineal into the heart at the same time and exhale on the outside through your heart. Feel yourself expanding through your heart, feel the connection and balance within your heart, and the connection with the spiritual realms of the cosmos and the earth.

Your heart is now filled with prana energy that creates a prana sphere around you. As you continue to breathe visualize the energy expands to encompass your entire body about 3 feet on all sides, above, below, front, back and on the sides. This prana sphere rejuvenates and nourishes your entire physical body and also activates the light body around you. The light body is called the MerKaBa vehicle (Mer –light, Ka- Spirit, Ba- Soul) which is your inter-dimensional vehicle as referred to in many ancient scriptures as the Chariot of God. The MerKaBa also represents the true nature of man in connection with the All That Is.

The Pranic breathing is our sacred connection to our multidimensional selves – our wholesome selves. We are not only physical material as a greater part of us is made of the formless – the material of the Spiritual realm; our true Home.

The Pranic breathing is a constant flow of goodness and wellbeing, sincere practice helps one to move beyond the games of duality. You can practice pranic breathing anytime, anywhere, while watching TV, or driving your car, or while working. Especially where there is discord in a particular situation or place do the pranic breathing to bring balance and protection. Become a conscious breather, a conscious participant of existence.

Practice continuously so that it becomes your habit, in such a way that it becomes your nature and occurs without any effort. Relaxing into the Prana, you understand that life can be lived effortlessly with ease and grace. Blessings!

It is vital to begin your day with pranic breathing and continue to practice this many times during the day. You will be amazed by the peace, harmony, and the excellence that you continue to create in your life through this.

End each day by using the rose tool to bring back your energy to yourself and also to give back the energy of others in your space. Clear yourself of mental clutter before retiring to bed. Relax in the heart space of Unconditional Love.

∞

Eileen Siegel Bowen

7 COMPASSION

"Sympathy is not compassion; it is just the opposite. Sympathy is a kind of exploitation of the other person. When you sympathize with somebody, you are higher, better, and the other is lower, falling, degraded. Your ego gets immense satisfaction out of sympathy. But this is how the unconscious mind functions. You don't know exactly what you are doing." ~Osho

COMPASSION – MEANING

The Merriam-Webster dictionary gives the meaning for compassion as the sympathetic consciousness of other's distress together with a desire to alleviate it. The compassion that is taught and understood on the Planet is sympathy or pity for another's suffering. Taking every effort to relieve another's pain is considered to be compassion. We have been taught that relieving the pain of others is good.

In order to go relieve another of their pain, the first thought that would come is a judgment with emotion. The judgment that the person is somehow suffering and that it is bad, and thus comes the judgment on the imperfection of creation. Projecting these judgments from the mind, one suffers with sadness. And sadness is an argument with God-Reality. If the meaning of compassion is to free others from suffering, how can we free others from suffering if we ourselves are already suffering with sadness for them?

When we project others' pain, we intensify their pain so much, and they would be much better without us adding more to their pain. So any person in pain does not need another suffering for them. The best person who can support them is the one who does not judge them or their pain. As parents, when our child starts to learn to walk, we see them fall many times; but do we tell them not to walk anymore because they are constantly falling? We trust that they grow only by moving through obstacles.

In 1996, Dr. Jill Bolte Taylor, a Harvard-trained neuro-anatomist, experienced a severe hemorrhage in the left hemisphere of her brain. She underwent a major brain surgery. She was very aware and awake during her stroke, and she went through a powerful 8-year journey of recovering from her debilitating stroke in complete awareness from a higher perspective. She recovered and came out of her ordeal with full insight into the greater purpose of life. She observed the play of energy around all aspects of life and shared her amazing experience in her book, *My Stroke of Insight*.

Viewing life from the perspective of higher truth, Dr. Bolte Taylor shares that when she was completely disabled and recovering, she saw that when people felt pity, sadness, or worry for her, they actually did not help her in any way, and in fact, they did the opposite. They sucked away even the little bit of energy she had. Hence, sadness or feeling pity is debilitating rather than empowering the person who is in pain.

"When we are being compassionate, we consider another's circumstance with love rather than judgment... To be compassionate is to move into the right here, right now with an open heart consciousness and a willingness to be supportive."
~Jill Bolte Taylor ~ *My Stroke of Insight*

∞

COMPASSION IS NON-JUDGMENT

Every sadness, anger, or fear for others or ourselves fragments our Spirit and we are not in the place of our power. When we are not in the place of our power, we tend to use our emotions positively or negatively. For a long time, we have been playing this game of powerlessness on the planet. Yet there is nothing wrong here; this is a game of duality on the planet where every emotion of powerlessness seeks greater solutions and expansion of wisdom and consciousness for the individual.

True compassion is a state of being in deep awareness of the situation and being in a place of total non-judgment. Without holding the consciousness of unconditional love, one cannot reach or even comprehend about compassion. Compassion arises out of unconditional-true love. All ancient scriptures talk about the unconditional love and compassion of

God. Since we forgot to live in union with our Divine Presence, we have divided ourselves from ourselves, and this division has lead to the loss of the wisdom of compassion.

It is true that our painful experiences make us stronger – we learn most from our pain. To know compassion, let us analyze what suffering is. Real suffering is not the temporary experience of being angry or frustrated, being incapable of action, or even the lack of being heard or understood. True suffering is when we cannot see the purpose behind the thing; when we are not able to understand the bigger picture. Due to the fall in consciousness, we have created a vast chasm between the Divine and us, and we have forgotten our wisdom. For thousands of years, we have been seeking knowledge but not wisdom. We chose to experience living from the mind and fell from our hearts into the mind.

The mind chooses logic and knowledge. The things of the heart are wisdom, understanding, and compassion. The mind is a storehouse and knowledge is easily available through books, teachers, the library, and experience. Knowledge is a memory of all things learned from the outside.

Wisdom cannot come from knowledge; wisdom comes from the love, kindness and understanding of the heart. Knowledge and cleverness have successfully helped to create a world of chaos and confusion. The world needs kindness and gentleness more than cleverness NOW. The wisdom from compassion is the greatest transformer for humanity and the Planet NOW.

When every aspect of life is dealt with from the place of compassion, it is possible to dissolve every kind of discord.

When every family unit, every social organization, education system, religious places of worship, institutions, and prisons become classrooms to aid people to connect with the heart and act from the place of compassion, we will be able to anchor inner Peace and thereby bring Peace on Earth.

∞

COMPASSION THROUGH AWARENESS

Until our spirit is wholesome, we will not be able to understand compassion. When our spirit is fragmented in anger, desire, and fear we can only feel the same fear, anger and desire in others. This leads to sympathy or empathy, but never to compassion. Compassion happens when the Spirit is wholesome, and when there is complete awareness of the Divine orchestration of life. Practicing to connect with the energy of our Spirit and the wisdom of our Soul, we come into the greater understanding of all things (Pranic breathing explained in the previous chapter is a grand practice to connect with our wisdom).

Instead of trying to understand from the mind, we allow ourselves to be in the place of pure awareness by conscious connection with our Divine Presence from our heart. Compassion has its origin in the heart space – the place of Divine Equality of All beings. People need to go into their hearts and find out for themselves.

Entering the heart can happen only through awareness – let every emotion rise, and let there be awareness in every emotion. Being aware in every moment, is like experiencing oneself as the infinite sky. The clouds of anger, fear, or desire come and they go, the sky is aware of them, but does not attach to them. The clouds are passing, they always pass, and they do not stay.

True creation happens only from the heart and not from the mind. Many scriptures and Great Masters have said that we are pure souls, and that this physical experience on the Planet is for our soul's growth. This truth gives value to all experiences whether they are positive or negative. From the mind, we may ask how can a negative experience have value. I am reminded of the time the tsunami hit India in 2004. Many people I knew were given the opportunity to see destruction right in front of their eyes. These people, as I know them, were pretty much asleep; they went about their lives from their minds totally playing the game of desires, achievements, comparisons and competitions. When they were given the first hand opportunity of seeing the tsunami and its devastating effects on the people and the land, their hearts opened in awareness. They changed their perspective on life 360 degrees. Now they value life so much that they share their time, energy, and money freely; they started viewing their wellbeing as the wellbeing and highest good of all concerned. I could see and feel it through their actions, words, and the mail they send to me.

∞

THE TRUTH OF OUR PRESENCE

Bringing our Divine Presence consciously into every aspect of life is an act of bringing HEAVEN ON EARTH. We are the Presence – expressing itself as a human being.

The Presence is the Sacred Observer – the Sacred Witness to every aspect of life. The Presence can be known by being alert, awake, and connected in the Present moment. We are a timeless, infinite being of immense magnificence and beauty. We love our infinite expansion, we love to go and experience the farthest, and the deepest. In our quest, we chose to enter into this experience called human form, ..space, ..time, and all limitations that are involved with it.

We are the ocean, and sometimes we like to experience ourselves as the wave. The wave rises, but falls back to become the magnificent ocean. Yes, being a human is a dream to experience limitation in order to more deeply and know our magnificence. The mind is the tool that holds us in this dream called human form, ...time, ...space, and we think that we are trapped and that we are hostage. But it is possible to wake up from this dream of humanity.

The powerful truth is that we are the Pure Awareness of the Divine Presence; we do not need to make awareness happen. We walk, we eat, we breathe with the body. Yet when we start listening with alertness to our walk, to our eating, to our breathing, it becomes the meditation that wakes us up from the dream of separation. Awareness makes us realize that the watcher, the infinite, the timeless Presence, is who we are. Let the Presence of the Silent Watcher be in everything we do. Every human is responsible to wake up from this dream. And the awakening can happen only by awareness.

When the mind is full of thoughts about complications and suffering, pull yourself out of it by practicing listening, feeling, and noticing. In silence, see the beauty of nature, feel the breeze touching you, listen to the voice of the birds, and the sounds of children playing. Do not think about it, allow awareness to happen, just be there, and just be aware. And in that moment, walks in the wisdom of the timeless part of YOU. When you get to know the timeless part of you, the experience of the You in time and space flows with ease and grace.

∞

OUR RESPONSIBILITY

"Take responsibility for the energy you bring." ~Jill Bolte Taylor ~ *My Stroke of Insight*

The consciousness we choose to hold about people and things is what we reflect on the outside. This world is our mirror, and it reflects what we hold on the inside. We are given the responsibility to choose the energy we bring to this Planet through us. It is very important to be aware of our mind and its stories. If we choose to feel sad or angry about the situations around us, we take part in aggravating the situation even more. If we choose to rise above our mind stories and trust in the benevolence of the Divine, we create peace, harmony and greater solutions for the situation.

We humans as a collective have forgotten our responsibility because we are fast asleep. We forgot that we are responsible for our reality. We are the ones who create our reality. We chose to be asleep and allow others to take our power and run our lives for us. For everything and anything we search for answers outside ourselves, and we have stopped relating to the wisdom of our inner beings. From religious teachings to all forms of knowledge, we rely on things on the outside. We have become so lazy that we accept what has been processed, reprocessed by others, and handed out to us as truth. This has imprisoned us into belief systems, all kinds of fear, and hopelessness.

Life is not the difficulty; However, it is the images created in the mind (the thinking) about the situations of life that make it difficult. There is nothing depressing in the world as every person is being the way they are meant to be at any given time. The concept of imperfection can be only in the mind that compares what is with what isn't. Choosing to believe our mind stories, we continue to view others and ourselves as victims and try to heal the pain by pitying and trying to *save* those who suffer. Our mind stories portray this world to be broken, and we believe that we need to sacrifice and save this world. Attaching to this perception from the mind has made us forget our divinity; we continue to scare ourselves with greater mind stories of imperfection, and we suffer by losing our joy. We continue to place roadblocks of fear in our life path and in that of others. Forgetting to trust the Creator's eternal goodness, we take over the work of saving a broken planet by getting into the business of our children, our neighbors, our coworkers, strangers, and the world at large. This has resulted in the creation of extreme stress, chaos, and confusion in the world. The things of the world cannot frighten us, only we have the power to frighten ourselves through our mind stories. How can we order God around when we can only see what is in front of us? We do not know the bigger picture, and we do not even know if life or death is good at this moment for us or for anyone else.

Responsibility is the ability to respond to life situations from our heart. The first act of empowerment is accepting responsibility for our life. It means taking responsibility for our happiness, for our health, for our wisdom, and for our creations. Human beings are a grand part of creation. Each human is built-in with powerful tools to create their part of Heaven on this Planet. The God-within every human heart, is a guiding light of immense love. Connecting back to Divine Oneness, lightens the grander path of life. Religion or rituals on the outside cannot reveal this to us; only by connecting to the divinity within will this grander path be revealed. This is what many great masters and teachers experienced and have shared as the KINGDOM WITHIN.

In the words of the Tao:

"Let go of fixed plans and concepts, and the world will govern itself."

Everything in reality as it appears to us in this moment is full of benevolence. The way to get out of our pain is to practice awareness and conscious connection to our Divine Presence. This keeps us in the place of total non-judgment. This simple way brings us wisdom to handle the given situation as there is no need to seek for it on the outside. In moments of pain or stress, it is our responsibility to be in awareness and ask Spirit to help us see the bigger picture, to literally start looking for the gifts in every situation, and to trust in the eternal goodness of existence. This brings the greater understanding that what we need at any given moment is already present and that there is no need to put the world in order for things are already in order. When we go beyond the mind, our way is clear. Doing what is required for the next moment without any argument is the grandest devotion to the Divine.

∞

COMPASSION OF GREAT MASTERS

Every great Master who has visited this Planet knows that we are grand co-creators with the Universe. It is our birthright to create life effortlessly by living in our hearts and holding the joy of the spirit. Every teaching of these benevolent masters was a reminder to live from our hearts and view the world from the place of non-judgment, and to live and breathe every moment in conscious connection with all life. Many of the Great teachers and Masters were able to perform miracles and heal people while holding their consciousness of non-judgment and complete trust in the eternal goodness of existence. They constantly reminded us that every one of us was gifted with powerful tools to transform our lives and that everyone can do the things they do and even more. There is no one to save, nowhere to go, and nothing to do. It is important to rise above the fear stories of the mind and to look at the world from our heart.

∞

THE OUTCOME OF COMPASSION

The outcome of compassion is transformation of the world into Heaven. We are born with the tools to empower the world and ourselves; therefore, the authors' intention of writing this book, is not to teach anyone anything. This book is written in the complete knowing that every human is born with the tools for transformation. This book is just a reminder through words. When one reads words that are a match to the knowing of the inner being, it is easy to sort it all out on the outside.

I am reminded of the story of *The Bishop's Candlesticks* from Victor Hugo's epic novel, *Les Miserables*, which is a grand portrayal of compassion and its outcome.

The story of *The Bishop's Candlesticks* is set In 19th century France. A prisoner, Jean ValJean, had spent 19 years in prison for stealing food and attempting escape. After his release from prison, he roamed from town to town looking for work. But because of his criminal past, no one offered him a job.

Hunger and tiredness drove him to seek refuge at the bishop's house. The bishop was known for his compassion, hence Jean decided to ask for food and to stay for the night. The bishop lovingly invited Jean and offered him food and lodging. The bishop's friend who was with him advised him against letting Jean stay for the night, but the bishop would not hear of it. Jean noticed silver candlesticks on the altar at the bishop's home, and he stole them when the bishop was asleep and left the house. However, the night guards caught Jean, saw the candlesticks in his possession, and brought him to the bishop's place in the morning. The Bishop said that he had given the candlesticks to Jean to sell so that he could move on in his life. The guards apologized and left Jean with the bishop. Jean cried and apologized to the bishop. The bishop told him to sell the candlesticks and to make an honest living for himself.

The bishop's friend asked him why he had lied to the guards, for which the bishop replied that in his heart, he had already given the candlesticks to Jean ValJean. The novel goes on to say that Jean ValJean ends up becoming a repentant, honorable, and dignified man. He becomes the wellspring of kindness for the people of the land.

Placing our awareness on our heart connects us to our God Within as our heart is the gateway to Universal Wisdom.

The physical experience of conscious breathing and bringing the pressure and warmth of the hand on the heart, opens the heart and allows us access to our Spiritual Home – our Kingdom Within.

Experience this moment now, bring your hand to your physical heart, and take in a deep conscious breath releasing it with a sigh or a sound. This connects you powerfully to your heart space, which holds understanding, wisdom, and awareness.

Practice being in this moment, this moment of the heart space, and you will be amazed by the transformation that happens to you.

Practice for the enrichment of energy and transformation; practice whenever there is worry or anxiety, and when you need a solution to a problem. As you continue to work with your heart, you will naturally connect with your Divine Blueprint, your Divine Wisdom, and your Divine Light.

Living in conscious connection with the heart is true living – life flows effortlessly with ease and grace. The wisdom of the heart teaches us that the earth does not belong to us, but we belong to the earth. Our bodies are sacred connections to the earth and the heavens. We are in this body at this time to bless the earth and our fellow beings with compassion from our heart. As humanity, we are here to manifest heaven.

In the words of the Native American Chief Seattle:

Every part of this earth is sacred.
Every shining pine needle, every sandy shore,
every mist in the dark woods,
every clearing and humming insect is holy.
The rocky crest, the meadow,
the beasts and all the people,
all belong to the same family.
Teach your children that the earth is our mother.
Whatever befalls the earth befalls the children
of the earth.
We are part of the earth, and the earth is a part of us.
The rivers are our brothers; they quench our thirst.
The perfumed flowers are our sisters.
The air is precious, for all of us share the same breath.
The wind that gave our grandparents breath also receives their last sigh.
The wind gave our children the spirit of life.
This we know, the earth does not belong to us.
We belong to the earth.
This we know, all things are connected.
Like the blood which unites one family, all things are connected.
Our God is the same God, whose compassion is equal for all.
For we did not weave the web of life.
We are merely a strand in it.
Whatever we do to the web, we do to ourselves.
Let us give thanks for the web and the circle that connects us.
Thanks be to god, the God of all.
~From an oration of Chief Seattle,
Native American, U.S.A., 19th Century.

∞

SPIRITUAL TOOLS

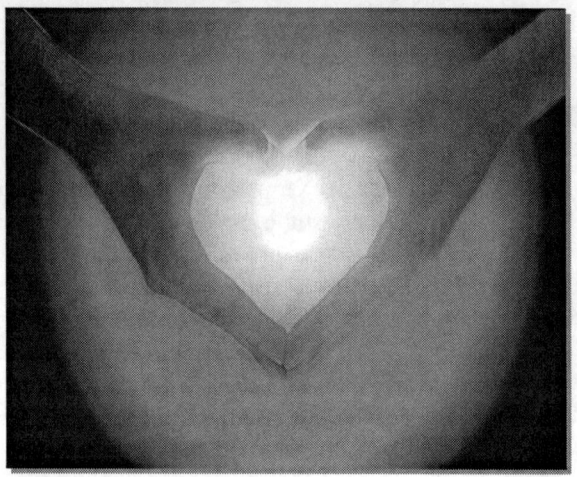

OUR HEARTS ARE HUGE TRANSFORMERS
~*A Heart Meditation* ~

The Creator breathed creation into existence. We are deeply connected by our breath with each other and with all of creation. This ocean of air is the world's heart. It holds all of the joys and all of the darkness that has been thought, felt, or said through the ages.

The purpose of entering the Planet as human beings was very well planned from the soul level to bring in mercy and blessings to the Planet. We are beloved children of the Universe, the Universe cherishes us, loves us, and adores our love in return. We are powerful beings with an amazing heart that can transform negativity into joy.

Negative thoughts and feelings do not disappear; they become forms and stay in the atmosphere. And when we live unconsciously, we are affected by the thoughts that are not even our thoughts.

Our HEARTS are huge transformers – they are huge wellsprings of compassion. Our hearts have the capacity to breathe in the entire world's suffering, transmute it with compassion, and breathe out benediction and joy into the Planet. We have the power to transform all pain into love!

The research conducted by the institute of HeartMath on heart-mind interactions, has shown the electrophysiology of intuition. It states that we are all globally interconnected at a deep, fundamental level through our electromagnetic fields and biofields. Their studies also demonstrate that it is possible to intentionally alter one's emotional state through heart focus. This research suggests that as people experience sincere positive feeling states, in which the heart's rhythms become more coherent, the changed information flow from the heart to the brain may act to modify cortical function and influence performance through a significant shift in perception, increased mental clarity and heightened intuitive awareness.

The heart is the most powerful generator of electromagnetic energy in the human body, producing the largest rhythmic electromagnetic field of any of the body's organs. The heart's electrical field is about 60 times greater in amplitude than the electrical activity generated by the brain. This field, measured in the form of an electrocardiogram (ECG), can be detected anywhere on the surface of the body. Furthermore, the magnetic field produced by the heart is more than 5,000 times greater in strength than the field generated by the brain, and it can be detected a number of feet away from the body, in all directions. This research illuminates the intriguing finding that the electromagnetic signals generated by the heart have the capacity to affect others around us. Their research indicates that one person's heart signal can affect another's brainwaves, and that heart-brain synchronization can occur between two people when they interact (http://www.heartmath.org/research/science-of-the-heart/head-heart-interactions.html).

The capacity of our hearts are enormous. Physically, the strongest muscles in our body are the muscles of the heart, and they are the first to form before any organ is formed in the womb. We literally begin life as OUR HEART!

We have been so long living from the mind and our senses that we never thought of connecting or living from our hearts.

Inhaling breath into the heart and exhaling out through the heart, brings an enormous calming effect. When we practice this art, we will discover our inner magician – the magic of the inner healer within us.

We do not need to breathe in love all the time as our hearts have the power to transform pain into love. As benevolent beings of unconditional love, we can breathe in the suffering of the world into our heart and breathe out joy, blessings, and mercy to the Planet. In practicing this HEART MEDITATION of compassion, we tap into our own healing energy, and we discover our inner magic. We become fearless and start feeling a tremendous connection with the world. The earth transforms wherever we are; it is literally like making deserts bloom into a lush green garden. Heart Meditation can be done anytime and anywhere by placing the awareness on our heart as we breathe.

This Heart Meditation is a most powerful way of bringing HEAVEN into our life and this Planet. Let us choose to bless our beings, our home, our Planet, and build Heaven on Earth!

∞

A PRAYER FOR COMPASSION

"Love and Compassion are necessities... not luxuries.
Without them humanity cannot survive." ~His Holiness the Dalai Lama

The Great I am Presence is within every soul. Living in union with our I AM Presence brings much compassion and clarity about our mission here on this Planet. This is a beautiful I AM Lord's Prayer as channeled by Elizabeth Clare Prophet. Reciting this Prayer every day and many times during the day, brought immense clarity and compassion to my life personally.

~The I AM Lord's Prayer~

Our Father who art in heaven,
Hallowed be thy name I Am,
I AM Thy Kingdom come,
I AM Thy will being done,
I AM on Earth even as I AM in Heaven,
I AM giving this day daily bread to all.
I AM forgiving all life this day even as I AM also all life forgiving me.
I AM leading all men away from temptation, I AM delivering all men from every evil condition.
I AM the Kingdom.
I AM the power and I AM the glory of God in eternal, immortal manifestation,
All this I AM.

CONTINUE TO PRACTICE WRITING THE GRATITUDE JOURNAL EVERYDAY…

∞

> "There is no coming to consciousness without pain. People will do anything, no matter how absurd, in order to avoid facing their own soul. One does not become enlightened by imagining figures of light, but by making the darkness conscious."
>
> ~Carl Gustav Jung

8 AWARENESS

"Earth's crammed with Heaven,
And every common bush afire with God;
But only he who sees, takes off his shoes,
The rest sit round it and pluck blackberries."
~Elizabeth Barrett Browning

"Your vision will become clear only when you can look into your own heart. Who looks outside, dreams; who looks inside, awakes."
~Carl Jung

"Life is only an opportunity to grow, to be, to bloom. Life in itself is empty; unless you are creative you will not be able to fill it with fulfillment. You have a song in your heart to be sung and you have a dance to be danced." ~Osho

∞

HEAVEN ON EARTH

In this moment there is Heaven on Earth; this is the truth of life. Only the present moment reveals the truth of life. The present moment reveals that we are love and the present moment reveals the Divine Presence. The powerful truth is that there is no life outside this present moment.

The past, the future, ideas, concepts, opinions, dreams, and fantasies are illusions created by thinking – thinking into a world of time. Humanity is lost in this created world of time that is an illusion. Most are unconscious of this, and many do not even care to inquire into it. Awareness is waking up from this world of time – the world of human thinking.

The ego mind is constantly working and taking us either to the past or to the future through the portals of thought. The mind does not know the present moment. If we continue to attach to our mind stories of our past, our future, our opinions, our concepts, and our ideas, we get lost in the world of dreams and illusions. Our absorbed attention into the beliefs about our mind stories completely disconnect us from the truth of life at this moment.

Giving attention and attaching ourselves to this illusory world of thinking, has the danger of bringing in the wounds of the past, our limiting beliefs, opinions, ideas, and our thoughts about the future. By focusing and attaching to this illusory world of thinking, we are projecting it onto the now moment, and we distort the gift of the now moment. The world seen though this distortion is extremely painful. It is the pain of separation from our truth, our love, and our Divine Presence. To ease this pain of separation, the mind constantly drives us to seek love, approval, appreciation, relationships, and success through mind games.

Awakening to the truth of life can be revealed only in awareness of the present moment. Every human is born with the capacity to wake up and live consciously. Awareness arises as we inquire into the truth of who we are and why we are here at this time.

The choice to be in the here and now opens us to awareness, and just relaxing into the now moment reveals the truth of being a conscious witness of all things. Here you witness yourself in this moment, you also observe your thoughts, opinions, dreams, concepts, and stories of the past and the future. You witness them, you do not get lost in them because you do not believe any of these stories and you do not project them on to the present moment. You are here and nowhere else, and you are not traveling in your thoughts somewhere. You learn to be here completely and absolutely available with the person, with the situation, with the room, with the tree, or with whatever is in front of you. By being the sacred witness, the holiness of life is revealed to you. You experience yourself as the love that you are. You experience the present moment as the truth, and you experience the Divine Presence revealed through this moment.

Our complete presence in the now moment is a grand gift for it will also call the presence of others around us. This waking up from separation with life makes an enormous difference to living. We experience our expression and expansion every moment, and our awareness makes us become very alert. If there is a slight discord with life, the witness takes note of it and harmoniously balances us back to integrity and Divine Presence. This is a beautiful way of living where there is no need for laws on the outside. This is the lawlessness of life.

Awareness allows one to experience oneself as love in existence with the God within. The realization that there is absolutely nothing in it and just silence as nothing belongs to you. It is the realization that there is nothing to do, no one to be, nowhere to go, no meaning to decipher, and no suffering; it is pure benevolence, living as peace and compassionate generosity. This is waking up to the truth of life rather than being lost in a dream.

Awareness brings the realization of heaven on earth; it helps us to see that life is a blessing. This present moment is heaven on earth, but we do not live here because we are so caught up with the world of time. We want to escape the present moment by being lost in the world of dreams and fantasies.

Living in awareness, we recognize ourselves as the caretakers and the guardians of life, and what we create complements life each moment. But living in our minds, everything we create is out of harmony with the truth. The disharmony leads to our end. The only hope we have now is by awakening to who we really are. It is our destiny to wake up, but the choice is ours. Let us choose to wake up now.

∞

AWARENESS IS WAKING UP

Before practicing any spiritual tools, the first and foremost step toward the journey of inner peace is awakening. It takes just a moment to awaken and from awakening, we move on to practice other spiritual tools of affirmations, visualizations, and prayers.

All creatures except man are highly aware of themselves and their environment. It was noted that whenever there is a tsunami in a particular place, except for the animals that were caged or tied, all other birds and animals migrated from that place to safer places well before the tsunami actually hit.

The book *The Secret Life of Plants* by the authors Peter Tompkins and Christopher Bird (1973) explores the fascinating relationship between plants and man. They showed that plants have the ability to detect human thinking.

In 1966, Cleve Backster, a polygraph expert, had playfully hooked up his philodendron plant to his galvanometer in his office to notice what kind of reaction the plant showed to its environment. He was holding a hot cup of coffee in his hand and decided to dunk one of the plant's leaves into it. As there was no reaction on the galvanometer, he then began to think of a more serious thing of burning the leaf with a match from his pocket, and surprisingly, the galvanometer reading went wild. This reaction on the machine led him to perform hundreds of experiments involving plants that revealed that plants were highly tuned to the movements of humans and animals (James Redfield in his book *The Celestine Prophecy*).

Even at the cellular level, all created things are alert and aware. Dr. Backster's experiments with human cells were mind-boggling. These experiments revealed that all living cells have a cellular consciousness and are able to communicate with each other even when they are distantly apart. In one experiment, he had isolated white blood cells from his saliva and kept them in a test tube connected with gold wire electrodes to an EEG type instrument. He was then searching for a sterile lancet to make a small cut at the back of his hand to obtain some blood cells. When he came back, he took a glance at the chart that was recording the electromagnetic activity of the white blood cells in the test tube and found that they had registered intense activity during his search for the lancet. His white blood cells were reacting to his intention to his cut hand even before he inflicted the cut (http://www.livepsyche.com/blog/spirituality/beyond-the-five-senses/biocommunication-ability-2/).

Dr. Cleve Backster further researched with cells and DNA with the U.S. Army. His Research has shown beyond any reasonable doubt that human emotion has a direct influence on the way our cells function in our body. The U.S. Army took DNA samples from a donor, put them in a room hundreds of meters away, and then had the donor watch emotional videos of war and love. When the donor experienced high and low emotions, his cells and DNA also showed powerful electrical response at the same instant in time.

In his book, *The Divine Matrix*, Gregg Braden concludes that this experiment has revealed that there is a previously unrecognized form of energy that exists between living tissues.

The Cells and DNA communicate through this field of energy and that human emotion has a direct influence on living DNA. Surprisingly, physical distance appears to be of no consequence with regard to the effect.

It is very clear that the intelligent field of energy in the Universe connects all created beings. It is not the axe in the woodcutter's hand but the idea of the woodcutter to cut the tree that would affect the tree; therefore, if an animal is killed, the entire forest would pick up the vibration of the distress. There are no boundaries for this Universal energy; it is like the air we breathe. We all are energy beings, and we all are connected – there are no borders. Only man seems to be asleep to this truth. All ancient ideas of war and destruction are unconsciousness, for even if one person is affected, the entire humanity will live in distress. This is a proven truth. It is time for humans to wake up from this sleep of unconsciousness and to connect with their heart.

Dr. Paul Pearsall has elaborately explained about cellular memories and Spirit connection in his book, *The Heart's Code*. His book brings awareness to the fact that when organs are donated or shared, the cell memories and energies are also shared. All of the research on the heart has revealed that the heart energy is powerful and that it connects with the universal energies beyond space and time. Feelings from the heart are capable of bringing healing to the body and the mind. Feelings from the heart also leave the body, go out into space, and connect with our loved ones, our pets, and our plants. The intelligence of the heart is able to view the gift of existence. The heart energy is omnipotent. When we wake and become aware and connect with our heart, the heart conveys to us the deep wisdom of the universe.

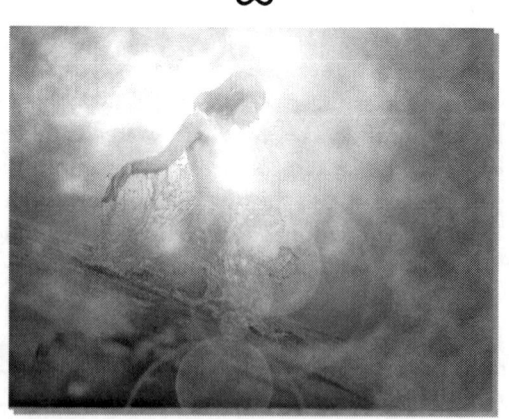

∞

AWARENESS OF UNIVERSAL ENERGY

Quantum physics states that this is a participatory universe. The abundant creative energies of the Universe respond to our expectations, and they are connected to human consciousness through intention. Every thought and feeling radiates from us in the form of energy fields that pour out into the universe and affect other energy fields around us. Our attention is awareness; it is energy through which we communicate with life. We have the freedom to choose to place our attention anywhere we like. The benevolent universal energies respond to our attention and co-create with us. This is why whatever we focus on magnifies.

Due to the fall of consciousness, many are unconscious of being unconscious. The few who came into this knowledge took advantage of the fallen human situation to gain power and control over the many as they learned to direct the attention of the masses on images of trauma, despair and destruction. The repeated focus of attention on words, pictures, and descriptions generate tremendous energy and thought forms from the masses that continue to create hopelessness and powerlessness on life situations.

Thoughts and feelings are very real and they have form. Our imaginations are powerful tools to create what we want in life.

All of the events of our life and of the planet are not random, meaningless acts. They are our unconscious creation due to lack of awareness. We are made up of both the physical and the non-physical material of the Universe, and according to the law of, "as above so below; as below so above," the universal energies support us in the creation of the collective ideals. The collective imaginations and agreements of all participants in the physical are supported in the non-physical and an energy structure is created according to the beliefs of the collective.

Being born into a collective consciousness on the planet is a powerful venture; it is a gift. Every individual affects the collective by their thoughts and feelings created by what they choose to believe at any given moment. Choosing to wake up and be in the place of awareness, in the present moment, is our gift to life.

This is the time of the birthing of a new humanity. A humanity that walks the planet in complete awareness. The cosmic intelligence of the Universe is constantly inviting us to wake up, to be aware and alert, and to consciously co-create with the goodness of the Universal energies NOW.

The innumerable crop circles, the meteor showers, solar flares, eclipses, and pole shifts are urging us to wake up to the truth of our connection to the Universe, and to be awakened to our power as being of peace and compassionate generosity.

Our bodies are intelligent tools that have been given to us to wake up to our power. Noticing our breath, connecting to our heartbeat, and viewing our world from the center of our head, are powerful ways to stay in awareness. Practicing pranic breathing connects us to the wisdom of our heart.

Albert Einstein stated that "We cannot solve our problems with the same level of thinking that created them." This is very true because we cannot change our reality from the same consciousness that made it. We must wake up and shift our consciousness toward what we want to create through being alert and aware in the present moment.

∞

KNOWING TRUE LIVING WHILE BEING ALIVE

Awareness is the key to true living while alive. Just because the physical body is breathing and the heart is beating, it does not mean that we are living. We are living only when we are aware of the breathing and the beating of our hearts and from this awareness responding to our environment with compassion. The world has forgotten to awaken. We have been asleep for so long that it feels more comfortable being asleep than being awake. But by being asleep, we are in a nightmare. To wake up from the nightmare or to live in the nightmare is absolutely each person's choice.

The nightmare of the planet today is the chaotic thought forms that are present in the energy fields of the Universe. They affect us and they alter our state of consciousness. Thought forms have the law of "like attracts like." Therefore, whatever we put our attention to, we will be absolutely supported by the energy fields. Our cells register all thoughts and commands and duly obey them. Unconscious thoughts and suggestions will often create damage to our body vehicles and our surroundings.

When we are awake and clear about what we need, we can consciously arrange our energy by sending intentions of nurturing and loving thoughts toward our surrounding environment and ourselves; thus we have a great part in changing the world in which we live.

Our thinking, feeling, intending, saying, and doing all create enormous frequencies on the energy fields around us. The practice of grounding and centering oneself assists to keep us in awareness, focused, and clear. Pranic breathing connects us to the wisdom of our heart, and we experience ourselves as co-creators. This helps us to be more conscious of frequencies around us. Through awareness we can detect and avoid discordance from our surroundings. Practicing and learning to accept our power as creators of frequencies, we can make wise choices to stop contributing personal fears and thoughts of powerlessness to the energy field. We can focus our attention in sending loving thoughts to the energy fields for peace and harmony for all forms of consciousness.

Living with awareness is powerful wisdom, and the world's indigenous people like the Native Americans, the Aborigines of Australia, the natives of Africa, India, and Central and South America, live in true awareness. They are the wisdom keepers of the planet. The civilized world may look at them and say that they are uncivilized. The civilized world has knowledge and technology to monitor the weather, to make machines to do the work, technological advancement in clothing, health, food, shelter and so forth. But the indigenous people need not depend on technologies to know about the weather, their body's health, their food, their water source, or to find their way through vast barren deserts without a map. They hold the wisdom of awareness and through awareness, they live longer, healthier, and peaceful lives. They even die or leave their bodies with awareness. It seems that once we fell in consciousness, we started creating technology outside ourselves in vague remembrance of the grand technology that lies undiscovered inside of us.

∞

KNOWING THE GIFTS OF EXISTENCE

I am reminded of the story of the beggar who sat near the seaside on an old rusted wooden box that he found near the sea. He put old newspapers and rags on top of it and made it his home. He sat on the box every day begging from the passers-by. Everyone knew him as he sat on the same place every day. He spent many years of his life begging for his living. People took pity on him and some gave him money while others brought him food or clothing. He accepted everything gratefully. It happened that one day he died in the night as he slept on his box. The next day the town's municipality came to remove his body. They also wanted to remove the box and clean the place. When they tried to move the box, it was very heavy. So they decided to break it open and remove the pieces. When they broke the rusted box, they found that the box was full of ancient gold pieces, coins, and other ancient treasures. If only the beggar had taken time to notice what was inside the box, he could have lived the life of a king.

Existence is a grand gift but by believing the stories of our mind about our situation, our past experiences, our future, our imaginations, our concepts, and our ideas, we build a huge wall of illusion around ourselves. We become blind to the gifts of existence. Awareness of the present moment dissolves the stories because the stories are everything outside this moment.

Belief in our stories have created a lot of repressed feelings of anger, hurt, sadness, pain, and need. These form the foundation from which we view our life. Limiting beliefs from childhood of "I am not loved, I am not wanted, I am not worthy, I can't do it, and I am not capable," go on a big list of things that support the story even more. We continue to live our life within our stories. Then we project our stories on to the present moment and judge everything in the moment based upon our stories. This creates a distortion about life, about love, and about us in general.

The stories take over every aspect of our life and prevent us from being our wiser, peaceful, and compassionate selves. The stories make us feel imprisoned with hopeless life situations. This then triggers us into making up more stories of a future that can bring us success or love;. Any ideal or goal to achieve in a future makes life more stressful because the future never comes as the future also becomes the now moment.

When we try to practice positive affirmations and follow the laws of attraction without first waking up in awareness, we continue to live within our story making it bigger and bigger. We can continue to improve our stories, but we cannot escape our stories.

Awareness is awakening out of our mind stories of the past and future, and out of the limiting beliefs that we have gathered from our childhood. In awareness, we understand where the truth of life is. We cannot stop our mind from thinking, but we can realize that we need not believe or attach our emotions to our stories. We need not feed or fix our stories, but we do need to wake up to know that they are stories and that we need not believe in them.

We cannot be in our presence all of the time; but we can practice to be aware and present just for one conscious moment, and to then add another moment and another moment to it. Thoughts are not under our control as the mind thinks without ceasing but by knowing awareness, we can understand that it is not necessary to believe the stories of our mind and suffer. Our stories make us seek for an awakening relief to escape from suffering; but we fall in love with our stories, and we strive to make them more pitiable so as to beg for love, support, approval, appreciation, or acceptance from the outside. When we do not get it what we seek, we then go back to create more stories. We get so very lost in the land of our stories.

The present moment with all of its gifts of heaven is waiting for us to wake up to our power. Everything in nature – the trees, the flowers, the breeze, the river, the animals, and the rocks are all inviting us to be here now. But we forget the present moment, and we travel into the world of time through our thoughts. As every thought boosts the ego, we have become addicted to this. Every mind story is about body-identification. We think that we are the body; therefore, every thought of the mind is about the body's survival, about its health, and about its comfort. Thinking this way, we stay limited, small, and separate from the rest of the Universe.

Life is too grand to be missed. It is completely filled with heaven, and it is possible for us to wake up to the present moment. Being fully engaged with mindfulness in the present moment is awareness as it brings silence. There is no story, and there is only the oneness of the now. When we understand that the present moment is awareness, we are one with reality. We see that whatever we have is what we wanted and that everything that life brings to us is good. We stop seeking, we stop taking control, we drop all illusions, and we let life live through us. We present ourselves as gifts, and we realize the beautiful gift that existence brings to us every moment.

∞

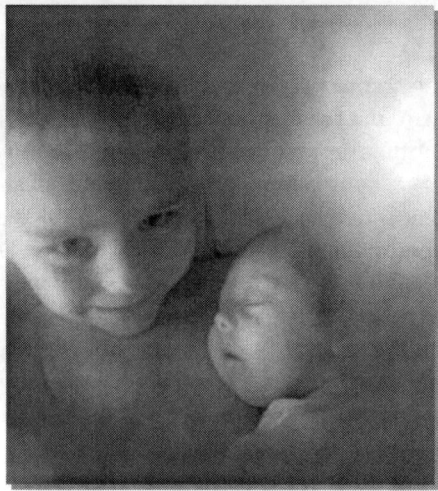

YOU ARE THE SACRED WITNESS TO LIFE

The only way to awareness is to be with the things of the present moment as a witness. Join the breeze, the voices of the children, be with the grass and the flowers, feel the chair that you are sitting on, or be with the dishes you are washing right now. Everything you do with awareness is ultimate success as it is perfect and you have lived that moment fully.

Practice to be present for just this moment – just be deeply present. This awareness of the present moment creates the space of silence and of stillness. Stillness is the key where life reveals its wisdom and truth. The Spiritual teacher, Eckhart Tolle, states that the entire wisdom of religion can truly be summed up in these few words:

"Be still and know I AM God."

Only in awareness and only when there is stillness, can true wisdom be revealed. When this moment of life is honored with mindfulness, the next moment automatically falls into place.

Awareness of the present moment brings oneness and connection with our eternal goodness as the illusions of our mind stories dissolve. The mind loves the ego stories and will never come to the present moment as the experience of awareness can never be understood from the mind. It is an experience to know the sacred witness of life. The sacred witness is the knower of all knowledge, ignorance, and wisdom. The sacred witness is the formless, non-judgmental self – our inner being. Awareness reveals the truth that all journeying and seeking of life is to recognize that the destination is WE-ourselves. The Hopi Elder's Prophecy, "We are the ones we've been waiting for," is a powerful reminder of this truth.

All stories of our past are not who we are. The mind loves this game of gathering information and clinging to identity and this becomes the heavy baggage that hinders our journey. When you come to the present moment, you understand that being in the present moment is a sacred witness expressing itself as a human being.

Noticing the sacred witness is the most powerful part of the journey of life. The journey of life when viewed from the sacred witness, allows understanding and comprehension of the stories of the mind and helps to make peace with them.

This world is our mirror, and the mirror reveals to us who we are in our story. Viewing our story from awareness and bringing in the energy of love, acceptance and compassion, we make peace with the story. We need not try to let go of the story; the story automatically lets go of us.

From the time the mind was born with the body, the mind took its job of safeguarding the body very seriously. Hence, it became a collector of every data from the outside, constantly alert, and constantly pessimistic. Its job is to scare us so that we do not go beyond its boundary. The mind knows only what it knows; it does not know anything beyond the data it collects.

Awareness is the simplest and most profound tool that reveals the truth that we are not our mind. Awareness differentiates us the as the watcher of our mind. We realize that we are much more than our mind; we are the magnificent miracle of life.

Just for fun while watching a movie or television, witness yourself watching, and notice the difference. The moment you witness yourself, you will not be involved in the drama happening in the television or the movie. You will SEE the drama only, and be amused as you will never get involved in it.

This is the way with awareness. It is the art of being a witness of the world around you every moment. You are a sacred witness as you see everything, but you do not identify yourself with anything that goes on around you.

Being the sacred witness is the most powerful place to be. From this place, we can see the beauty of creation, and we can see the drama chosen by each and every soul without judgment. From this place, we make peace with our stories by seeing them from a higher perspective. From this place, we understand that this world is a projection of our thinking, and we understand the world in a much better light. There is immense peace through this understanding, and we come to love the world and ourselves. After making peace with the story, we settle into our Divine Presence and emerge as a new being without limitation, without fear, and without concern about what others think. We become our authentic selves, and we create ourselves anew every moment. We reemerge as the sacred witness to life.

∞

BECOMING CONSCIOUS CUSTODIANS OF LIFE

From awareness we understand that this world is a *Hall of Mirrors* that perfectly reflects the consciousness we hold on the inside. Everything we see around us is our creation. Every responsible human comes equipped with a noble heart to take this journey of connecting back to his or her inner Self – the sacred witness.

We understand that our energy of attention is powerful and that it helps to create this physical reality. Let us stop to notice our thoughts, and let us be aware of where we are putting our energies right now. The creative energy of the universe runs within, through, and around all of us. We use this energy through our thoughts to create everything in our life.

You get an idea about making dinner. You focus your attention and energy on the idea, imagine the process of making dinner, and go on to create the dinner.

A sculptor looks at a stone and an idea appears. He focuses his entire attention and energy on it, and he creates a beautiful statue.

Unknowingly, we waste a lot of our creative energy everyday on things that we do not want. We focus on other people's business, their good and bad deeds, or we focus on the things that happened on the news. We focus on imagined fears about our loved ones and the list goes on. As we focus our attention on these things, the creative energy moves in that direction and creates more of what we fear and more of what we do not want or like. Unconscious identity with our mind stories has been very successful in creating chaos in our lives and on the Planet. It is time for us to wake up, be aware, and to exchange our unconscious identity for Truth.

Let us consciously participate in creating beauty, harmony, and peace. There is Heaven on Earth, we are the sacred witness of life, and we are the grand custodians of this Planet. Let us choose to wake up and be in the place of awakened consciousness, the place of stillness, and the place of understanding and wisdom. The more we connect with the heaven within, the more we see HEAVEN in our reality.

∞

SPIRITUAL TOOLS

Aligning With the Sacred Heart

According to the Pleiadians, Your Sacred Heart space is your whole chest area. To align with your Sacred Heart you must practice letting go and allowing the birthing process to bring you into the Sacred Heart space.

In aligning with your Sacred Heart space, place both hands flat on your chest. Feel the warmth and pressure of your hands on your chest, and bring your conscious awareness there.

Take a conscious breath and let it go into the space you are holding your hands to. Through your conscious breath you can allow yourself to feel the opening up of your Sacred Heart space. Continue to let go and use your conscious breath to assist you in entering deeper and deeper into this space.

Work with this process daily – gradually expanding and building into the opening of your Sacred Heart space. Each time you do this you are consciously aligning to your Sacred Heart connection…
~ The Pleiadians *via Christine Day*

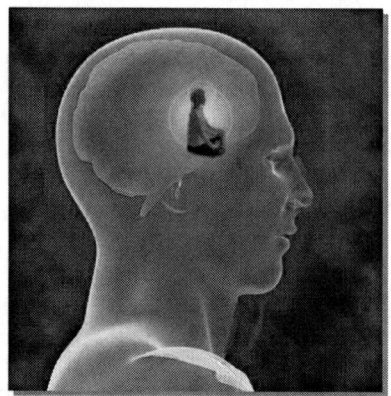

Looking at the World from the Center of Your Head

Sit in a straight back chair, place your feet flat on the floor, and close your eyes. Notice your breathing, breathe from your belly, notice your belly expand with every in-breath, and contract with every out-breath. Continue to breath in this manner.

Use both index fingers and touch your temples on either side. Notice where your fingers touch, and draw an imaginary line between the two points. Now move your hands 90 degrees to the right and touch the back of your head and forehead with your index fingers. Note the two points and draw another imaginary line intersecting the first line. Find the point where these lines intersect; this is the center of your head. Now remove your fingers and place your awareness in this place. You will definitely feel something here. This is because this is our place of power.

Your ability to imagine and visualize from the center of your head is your greatest tool. Imagination and visualization is energy work. When you are able to be in a quiet, undisturbed space, have centered, and think of it in your Spirit-Presence, then it already is. Being present with yourself, you are always in control. Energy work takes practice, but there is no right or wrong way to do energy work. When you are sincere and consistent in your practice, you will attain success.

Defining Your Space

From the center of your head, see your view screen with a red rose. See the rose as very real with soft petals, dewdrops on it, see a stem, a few leaves, and make it as natural as you have seen it in nature. The rose is a powerful energy tool of protection. You can keep a rose at the end of your aura and ask it to protect your energy field throughout the day. Visualize the rose between you and the people and the situations you interact with. The rose creates your boundary, you will stay in your space, you will not fragment your Spirit, and you will not hold other people's energies in your conscious or unconscious awareness. Holding other people's energies in your consciousness does not benefit either of you. You will be in your space and in your power. Practicing awareness becomes enhanced by this tool.

∞

HEALING THROUGH AWARENESS

The physical body is an expression of the spiritual. Higher Spiritual energy when it enters into the Planet gets translated into the physical. The physical body is influenced by the spiritual energy.

The body is a reflection that appears on the mirror of this Earth dimension. This body is the object and we as awareness are the subjects that influence the physical body. The physical world is a translation or expression of the Spiritual world.

The mind is not aware of such things for it runs on the information gathered from the physical senses only. The mind-ego cannot understand that physicality is only a reflection. It chooses to love or hate the reflection according to the data collected by the physical senses as its job is only to protect the physical body and it takes its job seriously. From this perceived illusion of physicality, the mind tries to physically get rid of all that it hates and to embrace all that it likes without any knowledge of the spiritual energy or consciousness that created the reflection in the first place. The truth here is that to heal or change the reflection, one has to connect with the consciousness that created the reflection to change it.

Healing Pain in the Body Through Awareness

There is always a tendency to react to pain from the mind; we search for painkillers to get rid of the pain. We never learned to be with our body or to communicate with our body's wisdom. It is a powerful experience to heal the body through awareness. Use this tool before you take any medication. It works remarkably!

Noticing that the breath consciously connects us to our spiritual energy, ground yourself, and place yourself in the center of your head. Now notice your breathing and take three complete breaths in and out.

Become aware of the spot where your body is in pain. From the center of your head, travel inward and reach the location of your pain. Notice the color, the texture, the smell, the temperature, or if there is any object sitting in the place of pain. Notice your breathing and be aware that your inner body atmosphere can be perceived totally. Use your creative imagination to heal and remove the pain from that place. For example, if you see dirt or dust there you can take a clean cloth from your pocket, clean the place, and then explode and dissolve the cloth into light particles. Or if you see the inflammation as red paint, you can take a cotton ball, allow the paint to be absorbed, and then explode the cotton into light particles. If you see objects blocking the place, remove them, and explode them into light. If there is too much debris, after sweeping and piling them up, see them explode into zillions of light particles. You may also take a jar of healing light and gently apply the light on the pain like a balm. Now notice the place as clean and free of inflammation.

Bringing the light of awareness is the most powerful healing for the physical body. The body craves for your attention and when you do not give it the attention it needs, it communicates with you in messages of pain or disease.

The moment we place awareness on the body the body rejoices and blossoms into its grander wealth of health, youth, and wisdom. Bringing the awareness of our Divine Presence to the cells of the body helps to awaken the cells to vibrate higher and illuminate in wisdom.

Placing awareness on the body is not only for times of pain so make it an everyday event. Visit with each part of the body one at a time – it may be a finger, a toe, an eye, or the nose. Travel inward into the body part and note all of the changes and differences. You can also breathe out love and light from your heart into that space and spread the light to all of the cells in that part of the body. Continue to practice and visit every part of your body and place your awareness to it. This exercise is so magical that you will soon notice your body transforming and glowing in youth, health, and wisdom as it shines with the light of the Higher Self. By bringing awareness to your body, you will have helped to remove darkness, lack, or limitation from your body and your environment, for the environment is ordained according to the consciousness held within the cells of the body. This is the art of enlightening your physical body as the self that has chosen to experience this physical plane; thereby, bringing harmony and peace to your world on the outside.

∞

9 MEDITATION~SILENCE

"Silence is the language of god, all else is poor translation."
~Jalaluddin Rumi

"In the silence of the heart God speaks. If you face God in prayer and silence, God will speak to you. Then you will know that you are nothing. It is only when you realize your nothingness, your emptiness that God can fill you with Himself. Souls of prayer are souls of great silence." ~Mother Teresa

"If we focus on the eternal, we will remain unaffected by the changing experiences of life." ~Sri Mata Amritanandamayi

"Meditation is the saving principle; it makes you immortal and eternal." ~Sri Mata Amritanandamayi

∞

THE SEARCH

There is a constant longing in the heart of man to experience something other than the physical. Deep within, every human longs to go home; home – to the heart of God. Throughout centuries, to seek this, many have climbed mountains, lived in the deep forests, made wilderness their home, underwent penance, followed rigorous discipleship, deprived themselves, fasted, and tortured their bodies.

The few who managed to taste the bliss of God have said that it is the art of effortless witnessing of life. You cannot find it anywhere on the outside, nor can anyone help you to find it. Only you have the power to find this bliss.

Any master, teacher of spirituality, or books like this one, can only share with you the experience. But to understand, implement the tools, and come to a conclusion is your personal journey. All knowledge and wisdom can be revealed to you only by keeping constant contact with the sacred witness.

Becoming a witness of life is meditation. Taking time to deliberately witness our actions, thoughts, and emotions helps us to realize that we constantly identify ourselves with our body and mind. The witness is neither the body nor the mind. This realization helps us to let go of all baggage of judgment, opinion, ideas, the past, and the future, for they all arise from body mind identification. This is true liberation.

We imprison ourselves in the stories of the past and the future. The access to past or future is only through memories and not anywhere else. It is okay to let go of the memories and liberate oneself. Our minds are amazing tools which hold memories stored in libraries of data about past experiences and future dreams. We can play with the mind, but it is not necessary to live there or get lost there in the world of time.

Only the Present moment can reveal the eternal oneness as it is where you truly find who you are and who God is.

∞

WITNESS LIFE

Witnessing life is effortless; it cannot be created nor imagined. Just pay attention to this moment, simply be here, do not try to control, see the thoughts come and go, you are not your thoughts, do not try to do anything, do not summarize or evaluate your feelings, and just be attentive to this moment only. Focus on listening within, there is no need to wait or expect anything as the moment you expect, you have flown away with your thoughts.

You cannot try to be aware, you are awareness itself. Allow the process to unfold within you. The body is present, and it is a beautiful tool to walk this earth life. The mind is present, and it is a beautiful tool to protect the body. But as you pay attention and listen, you understand that you are the sacred witness, the healer, and the alchemist of life. There is nothing to fix, change, or hold on to as you were never born, and you never die. You are simply there.

At one time my daughter, Sally, who was then entering her freshman year in high school, had to read the book, *A Child Called It,* for her assignment. The book shocked her, and she asked me to read the book along with her. The book was the most disturbing book that we had ever read. It was the story of child abuse in its most horrendous form. The author, Dave Pelzer, had shared his story as his alcoholic mother had abused him in the most horrifying way possible. *A Child Called It* was his autobiography. Reading the first few chapters of the book brought so much pain that we had to stop reading the book. Then we decided to read it from the place of awareness – being the sacred witness.

Being in the place of awareness, we were able to read the entire story peacefully from a place of non-judgment. We witnessed the victim-villain game being played constantly by the mother and the child. As the torture and starvation came to its peak, the child remembered the words of the "Lord's Prayer" that said, "deliver us from evil." He uttered the sentence with complete desperation. It just so happened that when he went to school that day, the school nurse noticed the stab wound and other wounds on his body. The nurse realized that he was extremely abused at home, and she called the social service agency. He was delivered to a safe place on that day.

It was powerful to witness that victim-villain games stop when we awake and say that it is enough. We are the power in our life. Situations in life are triggers that push us to wake up to awareness – to our power within.

Practicing being a witness of life is absolutely effortless. My daughter went on to write a beautiful summary for the story from a place of compassion. She was clearly able to see the mother who was so delusional with alcohol, and a child who awoke to be in his power. Witnessing is silent awareness, mindfulness, and attentiveness; compassion and wisdom arises out of that silence.

∞

THE GRAND ALCHEMY OF PRESENCE

Witnessing – being in our presence in the present moment, is an art of true living; it is meditation. It helps you to understand that you are neither your body nor your mind. The body is a beautiful tool to walk on this planet with, and the mind is made so beautifully that it can store, arrange, analyze, collect, inform, imagine, and evaluate. We communicate in this physical planet using our body and mind. The body and mind are a part of us, they do their job wonderfully, and it is our responsibility to use our body and mind wisely.

Meditation is a way of understanding the body and the mind. Witnessing the actions of the body and the mind is the most simple and effortless way of living as your true self, and living in your power. Every moment of life is an opportunity for meditation. Every act of life can be a meditative act. Grounded in the present moment, staying in the center of the head, and witnessing the actions of life leads to stillness. This stillness brings deeper understanding of life. When you are able to witness something, you understand that you cannot be that something as whatever you can watch, becomes separate from you. The body is more tangible and so can be easier to notice. When you get familiar with noticing the body, you can start noticing the mind.

Meditation is a constant act of noticing everything that is happening. It is noticing your body walk step by step. It is noticing while your hands help your mouth to eat, noticing your changing moods and emotions, and just being there with your wholesome self – just noticing. Noticing your walking you understand that the body is walking but not you, and by noticing your body in health or sickness, you understand that you are watching but you are neither your health nor your sickness. When witnessing, your powerful presence is capable of removing the cause of the sickness as you do not judge because you are not in the mind story. Therefore, the more you are in awareness that you are not your sickness, you are able to eliminate it altogether. Noticing your body in pain, you understand that it is the body's message but that you are not in pain. By placing wholesome awareness in the place of your true self, you understand the mind stories that have caused the pain. This realization brings your powerful, nonjudgmental presence to the situation, and the pain automatically dissolves. This is the grand alchemy of Presence.

All suffering arises by identifying oneself as the body and the mind. The act of meditation brings the light of understanding that one is neither the body nor the mind. Yet one is the eternal presence which notices the body and the mind. In the noticing, there is an alchemy happening, you become nonjudgmental, and you witness life as a most precious gift rather than mindlessly reacting to situations. We call this noticing mindfulness, and in being mindful, we take time to respond to situations from our true self. We bring in higher solutions and grander creations, and we become our authentic selves.

When we become our authentic selves, we trigger others around us to also be in their truth. However, some are not ready for it yet. We may find many people leaving as old friends and relationships that do not vibrate in harmony to our state of authenticity may move out of our life. Life will bring us people who walk their truth. Our fears turn to love and our loneliness becomes a more beautiful state of all-one-ness with the Divine Presence. There is a greater understanding of unity and oneness with all life as in truth, there is no separation.

∞

MEDITATION IS JUST A TOOL – THE ULTIMATE GOAL IS KNOWING THE TRUE SELF

Meditations are a tonic that help to release the mind of its chatter. Every aspect of life can be made into a meditation. When life becomes a meditation, the light of understanding and wisdom blossoms within us.

Each meditation is embedded with specific energies to enhance and magnify the focus of the meditation. Each session can take as little as three to ten minutes, or you can simply relax and enjoy the practice for as long as you wish. It is suggested that you start with one exercise and do it three times a day for a week before moving to the next. Try out all the exercises and find the one you feel expands you the most and customize it for yourself. These are just simple guidelines; the greater guide is always your feelings as you are the master of your life. You are the only one who can awaken you to your true self.

Ground yourself and be in the center of your head as you witness yourself. It is important to keep a gentle smile throughout and enjoy!

∞

WALKING

Take time to mindfully notice your feet, see how your feet move one after the other, and watch the swinging of your arms. Observe that in this moment your body is performing the amazing action of walking and helping you to move. Now look at the passersby. You are fully in this moment and there is no chatter in the mind. You will notice that surprisingly, you are more alert to everything around you. You slow down, and you enjoy the noticing. The noticing brings healing and awakening to the cells of your feet and strengthens your connection to the earth.

∞

BREATHING

Create a quiet place and sit comfortably. Start noticing your breathing; watch your breath move in and out of your lungs effortlessly. Follow the breath from the nostril to the lungs and back again continuously. You will notice that you are not doing the breathing and that you are actually being breathed. Hence, you are being lived every moment. The understanding of effortless living blossoms within you. The noticing brings healing and awakening to the cells of your nose, lungs, air passage and your blood, it strengthens your connection to the prana energy or life force energy of the Universe.

∞

Kit Alderson

CONNECT WITH NATURE

Sit with a tree or even a potted plant if you have one and observe its Presence in silence. Remember as a child how you were attracted to a procession of ants or a bug on a plant. Take time to follow the insects or birds that come to visit. If there is a pond with fish or if you have an aquarium at home, sit quietly and observe. You will find that your thoughts have magically stopped and that you are calm, peaceful, and more alert to life. The connection brings awakening to the wisdom of the Universe.

∞

EATING

Make it a practice to eat only when you are hungry and to drink water only when you are thirsty. To trust the wisdom of the body is a most important decision.

Our body is unique. Listening to our body and being aware of its needs and requirements is a grand decision. Every cell in our body holds the wisdom of the Universe and the wisdom of all previous lifetimes. When we decide to live in awareness with our body, we have made the profound decision to anchor wisdom.

The practice of using the pendulum to discern truth or for dowsing is a powerful practice that assists in understanding the wisdom of the body. People think that the pendulum has power but that is not the case at all. The pendulum receives its power from the wisdom of the cells of the body. The cells hold the wisdom of the Universe and when you ask a question and allow the pendulum to swing, the movement of the swing is propelled by the cells in the hand that holds the pendulum. And as the pendulum moves, the person's question is answered.

Eating food with awareness is a profound art of connecting with our body's intelligence.

Do not drink liquids along with your food. Water should be drank either a half hour before or after eating food – this is to allow the juices of your body such as the saliva, the juices of the liver, the pancreas, and the gall bladder to do their work perfectly without being diluted. For the sake of meditation, at least once a day take your plate of food with you and sit in a lotus position. Quietly sit away from television, radio, books, or talking with others. Lovingly touch your food and place small portions in your mouth. Follow your food in your mouth, take time to mindfully observe the food being ground in your teeth giving plenty of work for the teeth. Allow the food to be broken down and mixed completely with saliva before swallowing. Do the same with the entire plate of food. Only encourage the thought of the food. You will notice that if you maintain this practice, you will neither over eat not under eat. Your cells will be satisfied completely, you will not be hungry often, your weight will normalize, you will feel lighter, and your body will be healed. Also your mind chatter will have reduced.

∞

OBSERVING THE NIGHT SKY

Take time to go to a place where you can watch the night sky in silence. Look into the vast expanse of sky and the twinkling of the stars. You can even take a sleeping bag or mat, lie down under the open sky, and just watch. Be there; you will see yourself in oneness with the Universe.

∞

DOING NOTHING

Every day, take time to sit silently for fifteen to twenty minutes with yourself doing nothing. Just sit silently, observe your breath, observe your thoughts, and notice the world around you. If possible, do this exactly at the same time everyday in the same place. If this is practiced regularly, it will help to stop mental chatter, and you will awaken to your light of understanding.

∞

"When the Japanese mend broken objects, they aggrandize the damage by filling the cracks with gold. They believe that when something's suffered damage and has a history it becomes more beautiful"
~Billie Mobayed~

PRACTICING NONJUDGMENT

There is a practice in the Zen teachings of Japan that when they mend broken objects, they aggrandize the damage by filling the cracks with gold. It is a way of finding beauty and perfection in imperfection, and it is a way of training the mind to go beyond judgment.

It is the nature of the mind to judge and compare. It is nothing bad, it is just what the mind does, and it is the mind's way of analyzing things. It is good to notice our thoughts when we judge ourselves for judging. Being in the place of allowing and not attaching, the judgmental thoughts just pass by. Accepting, noticing, and allowing every judgmental thought in the mind is the kindest and gentlest way to find clarity.

A non-judgment meditation involves noticing the things we judge about others, and trying to feel it from that person's place. For example we can try doing simple things like writing or drawing with our left hand if we are right-handed or write or draw with our right hand if we are left-handed. We can visit a museum of art, look at the paintings and sculptures, and notice the rush of judgments that come to our mind. You can try looking at simple things like a rock, a flower, or a coin, notice the mind story, and let go the mind story. Then practice looking at the object without the story of good or bad. After practicing with objects, it will become easier to practice with people.

Take a broken vase, an unevenly shaped pottery, or a broken instrument and make a simple shift of perception through your creativity. You can take pictures of the broken object in different lightings, in different places of nature, or grow flowers in them. Find at least ten different ways of creatively looking at the broken object and transforming it by shifting your perception. This practice opens our mind and brings clarity to our vision.

Noticing ourselves judging, we notice that our bodies also react in a negative way to the judgments. Practicing to send blessings is one of the most powerful ways to move beyond judgments.

∞

PRACTICING BLESSING

In conscious connection with Divine Presence, graciousness happens. With graciousness comes the will to bless humanity and the planet. To bless means to sanctify or to make holy. To bless is to acknowledge and bring forth the eternal goodness of the Universe that is awaiting our call. It is the responsibility of every human to wake up to their power to sanctify and make holy all humanity and the Planet.

Living as a sacred witness in the present moment, the

holiness of life is revealed, we experience ourselves as the love that we are, and we experience oneness with the Divine Presence. Oneness brings the light of understanding that All is God, All is Good, and All is One. Blessing happens from the place of Unity and Oneness with existence.

In the beginning, it is enough that one practices blessing oneself and others from an intention for open mindedness and expansion. When awareness arises through the practice of witnessing, blessing becomes a natural habit.

Waking up in the morning, bless yourself for being a part of existence, bless the bed that gave you rest, bless the ground that you place your feet on, and bless the day that it may turn out to be wonderful for every being alive. While meeting people, bless them with wellbeing in all aspects of life, bless the birds, the animals, and the trees that you see around you. As you travel to your work, bless all the offices, schools, hospitals and government institutions that you may see on your way. Entering your office, bless the people there, bless your work, and your clients. Bless every situation you meet, for they are divinely orchestrated for you. When evening comes, bless and thank the eternal goodness that has created grandness in your life this day. Eternal goodness is our birthright, and it is our responsibility to allow it to flow into our lives and into the Planet.

It is impossible for blessing and judgment to share the same space. So the more we practice blessing with intention, the more we move beyond our mind stories. We experience the Divine Presence in us, and we attain inner peace.

∞

METTA MEDITATION – THE PRACTICE OF LOVING – KINDNESS AND COMPASSION

This is one of our favorite meditations.

METTA is a Pali word meaning loving kindness. The Buddha originally taught this meditation. It is a practice of mindfully cultivating love and kindness toward the self, loved ones, friends, strangers, and all sentient beings.

In this meditation, one recites specific words and phrases in order to apply generosity and kindness to all beings and as a consequence, find true happiness in another person's happiness no matter who the individual is.
Practitioners of Metta meditation offer this meditation for an hour or more; however, to start with we can do it for just ten minutes a day and still be blessed with immense happiness and peace.

The practice of Metta endows the Four Universal Wishes – to live happy, to be free from hostility, affliction, and distress.

This can be done as a sitting meditation everyday for ten minutes, and it can be done as a walking meditation during morning walks while blessing the Planet, or it can be done while doing chores every day. Many offer Metta for twenty minutes each evening just before bedtime.

Begin the meditation by taking a few moments to ground and center yourself and focus your attention on your breath. Start by offering Metta for yourself first.

Recite the following phrases to yourself in a pace that keeps you focused and alert:

May I live in safety.
May I be happy.
May I be healthy.
May I live with ease.

Continue reciting these phrases until you feel comfortable.

Now offer Metta to someone you know in this way. It may be a loved one, a friend. or neighbor. Visualize the person in your mind's eye and say:

May he/she live in safety.
May he/she be happy.

May he/she be healthy.
May he/she live with ease.

When your Metta has easily flowed to this person, offer Metta to a stranger (perhaps someone you met in the store), and then you may offer Metta to a difficult person in your life.

Now offer Metta to all beings (every man, woman and child on the planet, the animals, birds, plants, elemental beings, all beings above and below the earth, and all seen and unseen everywhere).
Your Metta can be offered this way:

May all beings everywhere live in safety.
May all beings everywhere be happy.
May all beings everywhere be healthy.
May all beings everywhere live with ease.
    Metta meditation, when practiced regularly, is powerful to release negative feelings and replace them with our true nature of loving kindness.

Easy Reminders

Meditation is the art of noticing, or witnessing life.
We can make every day situations into meditations.
Meditation helps to go beyond mind chatter and see the world from the place of non-judgment.
Practicing the art of witnessing, we meet our True Self – the Alchemist.
Every human is responsible to wake up to their True Self and bless the planet by living in awareness.

∞

10 CONSCIOUS CONNECTION

"Live each moment completely and the future will take care of itself. Fully enjoy the wonder and beauty of each moment." ~Paramahansa Yogananda

"Self-realization is the knowing in all parts of body, mind, and soul that you are now in possession of the kingdom of God; that you do not have to pray that it come to you; that God's omnipresence is your omnipresence; and that all that you need to do is improve your knowing."
~Paramahansa Yogananda

"Anyone seeking higher knowledge must create these feelings (Reverence, awe, adoration and wonder) inwardly, instilling them in the soul. This cannot be done by studying. It can be done only by living."
~Rudolf Steiner ~*How to know higher Worlds*

∞

HARMONY OF LIFE

When living in harmony with existence, every aspect of life becomes healthy. Spirituality is the ability to be in tune with existence and with the light of Love. The meaning of life in the physical is to develop the heart and the consciousness. The responsibility of every created being is to evolve. Our evolving is an integral part of the evolving of the Universe. Evolving involves conscious awareness and wholesomeness.

We are Spiritual beings living in multiple dimensions; however, we have focused our attention to this dimension to gather information through our physical experiences. Humans are multidimensional beings composed of multi-faceted parts with connections to many dimensions.

Pure Consciousness manifested itself into a body in order to experience physicality. The timeless brought itself into time and space. As soon as this was established, attention was focused on the physical and a new, limited, and restrictive consciousness "I am the body" was formed. The truth is that we are Pure Consciousness. Spirituality is the ability to return back to the Awareness of ourselves as consciousness from the physical experience. The physical body and the physical mind reflect the Light of consciousness, but they are a very limited consciousness.

To know and experience the truth of who we are from the limited physical consciousness, we go through the experience of who we are not. These are not negative experiences. These are experiences that awaken us to the truth of who we are, and when we inquire and dwell deep into the awakening process instead of escaping it, we bring grander solutions and greater wisdom. We birth ourselves into Pure Consciousness.

The harmony of evolving into Pure Consciousness is experiencing oneself as a Divine being in everyday reality. It is a process of loving and embracing every aspect of life without judgment and experiencing oneness and Unity with life. And from this Unity, choosing to live from the place of being happy, gracious, peaceful, compassionate, generous, and loving.

The restrictive consciousness of the body and mind bring in illusions to provide a playing field within which we can analyze, create, and evolve ourselves every moment. Our gathered experiences from the game of life create a data bank called the ego or the inner child. Within each and every one of us resides the inner child who is addicted to take on the job of protecting the body from harm. The inner child only knows itself as, "I am the body," hence it lives in constant fear. Healing the inner child in us with conscious awareness is the way to Self Realization.

∞

Shiloh & Anna ~ Dawn Haliburton-Rudy
INNER CHILD

The inner child is the data or memory keeper that lives inside us. The inner child is innocent, playful, creative, and unconditionally loving. The inner child believes that it is the body and it develops fear as a result of painful experiences. The painful experiences make the inner child to develop something called the ego whose constant focus becomes survival of the body. The inner child was created to safe guard the body, and by collecting and keeping memories it develops fear. If we are not aware of this, the memories create discord in life. The memories are projected on to every life situation and prevent us from evolving into the truth of who we are. It is the child on the inside that needs love and needs transformation through love.

The fear memories of the inner child begin at the time of

birth when we separate from the Creator – our Spiritual home and are born into a physical body. At the time of birth, the baby is separated from the mother's womb, which was so comfortable for nine months, and is exposed to harsh light, coldness, and sounds. Separation for the baby presents itself on many levels and as the child grows, there is more separation. All of this separation begins to form memories of fear and abandonment. The child grows and realizes the rules played in the physical world. Early in life through the dictates of the society and the people around him, the child learns to please others rather than himself in fear of rejection, punishment, or more separation. It is the mask we learn to wear every day. We strive to please others, to win approval, and in doing so, we hide our truth. The inner child comes to a realization that this world is not a safe place.

The fear to be perfect makes you hide behind a mask. The British sitcom, *Keeping Up Appearances*, jokes about the life of a middle class woman who is obsessed by perfection, image, and etiquette. Her obsession leads her to do foolish things and creates pain for herself and others.

Keeping up our appearance everyday is the mask we wear because of the fear of rejection. The inner child creates masks of things that it feels would not be accepted by society. In reality, we are not on this Planet to fulfill anyone else's agenda. We are here to evolve ourselves into our Truth and to achieve Self Realization.

> "I do my thing and you do your thing. I am not in this world to live up to your expectations. And you are not in this world to live up to mine. You are you, and I am I, and if by chance we find each other, it's beautiful. If not, it can't be helped."
> ~Fritz Perls ~*Gestalt Therapy Verbatim* (1969)

∞

HEALING THE INNER CHILD

The world does not begin from outside you – the world begins from you. You are the one who gives meaning to the messages received by your physical eyes, ears, nose, taste buds, and tactile senses of your skin. You create the world through your senses absolutely. The meaning for everything is the meaning you give it. You are the master of your creation. It is in your power to see it the way you want. Nothing outside you has the power to hurt, damage, or destroy you in anyway. If you perceive something as not good, then go inside and create it better. In order to change the picture on the outside, go within and change the perceiver on the inside.

This world is a perfect mirror – it reflects to us our deeper inner truth. We project our inner fears on to the world outside and we react to situations from our fear. Then we set out to heal the world outside, but the Truth is that we are the ones that need to be healed.

Dr. Ihaleakala Hew Len, is a Hawaiian therapist who cured a complete ward of criminally insane patients through a Hawaiian healing process called ho'oponopono. Ho'oponopono is the shamanic practice of forgiveness native to Hawaii. It explicitly encourages verbally forgiving one's own inner child and loving the self. With the technique of ho'oponopono, Dr. Hew Len healed the patients without seeing any of them. He took each of the patient's charts and looked within himself to see how he created that person's illness. As he continued to work on himself, the patients were healed. The work he did on himself was to say the words "I am sorry" and "I love you" over and over again. The simple technique of Ho'oponopono is to love the self and to forgive.

With the concept of total responsibility of creating our outer world from the inside, Dr. Hew Len teaches the art of taking total responsibility for the world we live in. Total responsibility means responsibility for everything in your life simply because it is in your life. The entire world is our creation – everything we see, hear, and touch is our responsibility just because it is in our life. Thus, everything outside is a projection from the inside world. If this is so, then everything good or bad exists because of our concepts on the inside. So the problem is not with the world outside; however, it is with the world inside, and to change that we must work on ourselves.

∞

TRANSFORMATION

When we take responsibility for our own creation, we are in the place of our power. When we make excuses or blame others, we are giving away our power. We constantly tell ourselves that we have no control over our life, our feelings, or our decisions. Blaming others holds us back from opening to our power within, and we cannot evolve into our authentic selves. No one can make decisions for us or think for us. We are completely responsible. By realizing our responsibility, we are in total freedom to choose to live our lives from the place of Truth and Love.

Love is the truth of who we are. Everything that we perceive as not love is an illusion that has risen from the concept of being not worthy. Feelings of unworthiness arise from a belief system from within. Choosing love is to come into the place of non-judgment and to be loving of every part of the self absolutely. Fear is the lack of love and every emotional reaction to life, which is not love, comes from the place of fear held in the memory banks. Whenever fear happens, our reaction is to push it away, to run away, to overpower it, or to hide. It is the hard wired fight or flight set in the mind to protect the body. It is also because this is what we have been taught to do. All of these negative, unconscious aspects that we have hidden are what run our lives most of the time, and this way of judging the self and waging war with the self or the world leads to chaos and confusion. Let us ease to adapt to being still and waiting to be shown the wise way.

Only when we take responsibility for our reality, can we transform it. We cannot transform what we do not own. Transformation begins by identifying our fears, and getting out of our mind stories of perfection. This is the first step to identifying our fears.

The outside world is our reflection. In reality we are standing in front of another version of ourselves; therefore, in healing me, I am actually healing others. It is only when we face things exactly as they are without any judgment that a light of understanding will be born out of the events. We hold so much fear inside our bodies. We fear failure, we fear success, we fear speaking our truth, we fear to commit, we fear to trust, we fear controversy, and the list goes on and on.

Fear makes us to hide behind a false personality. We beat ourselves down, and we give in to unreasonable situations just to go with the crowd or to please others. Bringing conscious awareness to our reactions toward life situations is the act of identifying fear. Processing the fear through love and acceptance brings transformation. Once we identify our fear, we can talk to our fear. We can ask ourselves what is the worst that could happen? We can ask if we are true to ourselves. We can ask what do we feel when we are not true, and what are we afraid of losing?

Thoughts continue to haunt us. It is a tendency for all of us to travel with our thoughts to the past or to the future. Past and future are only memories and concepts of the mind, and they are not real. The only thing that is real is you in this Present Moment. See yourself in this present moment as this is the only moment you have, and this moment is a grand gift. To be in this moment, just watch your breath as it moves in and out of your nostrils. Be there for some time, and observe that you are not even doing the breathing. It happens effortlessly, you are Present, and life lives you. Life breathes you, just watch, notice that you are the one watching, and you are not your thoughts.

You are being breathed and lived every moment effortlessly. Isn't that amazing?

We live before we come into this body. We now live in the body, and the body comes and goes, but we are eternal beings. We travel through space and time, we gather wisdom through every experience of the body, we expand our consciousness when we live our truth, we are continuously recreating ourselves, our reality is only a brief moment in time, we are the creators of our reality, and we are never born and we never die. When we question our fear and embrace it without judgment, we open our hearts and healing happens.

∞

LIFE FORCE ENERGY AND THE INNER CHILD

Every time we attach to our thoughts and work up an emotion, our life force energy is expended. Each one of us has an allotted portion of life force energy to spend per day to run our physical bodies. Our emotions move the life force in our body. Our beliefs and attitudes depict whether we lose energy or gain energy every day.

When we live from the place of fear and are constantly comparing and attaching our emotions to judgmental thoughts, we lose energy. When we continue to have a condemnatory nature, we lose heavy amounts of energy and we experience fatigue. The fatigue may affect us physically, mentally, or emotionally.

Since the inner child was created to be innocent, playful, in love, and in joy, every negative emotion that is of fear creates fatigue for the inner child. If we choose to spend more of our energies in judgments and negativity, we end up losing the daily portion of life force energy. Because of our negative attitudes, we are not motivated to connect with our soul or our spirit and hence, there is no more energy for the body from the Universe. The much needed life force energy is then taken from the tissues of the body, from the joints, bones, and the muscles causing physical and emotional pain. When we continue to deplete the body of much needed energy, we have to face the consequences. Our bodies become tired and weak. We become short tempered, more irritated, and we even stop doing the things we usually do. The inner child communicates this fatigue in the form of headache, back pain, or sometimes more serious illness.

The inner child reenergizes itself through sleep, laughter, play, and conscious connection with Spirit. Gossiping, making deliberate negative comments, and saying negative things to people drains an enormous amount of energy. Negative beliefs and judgments also expend a lot of energy. It is wise to notice when you are losing your energy and when you are gaining your energy.

There are seven energy centers in the body through which the inner child collects data related to life experiences. The life force energy also flows through these energy centers. These energy centers of our body are called the chakras. The word chakra comes from Sanskrit – an ancient Indian language. Chakra means vortex or a spinning wheel of energy. The ancient people of India believed the chakras to be major centers of spiritual power in the human body that store, distribute, and balance life force energy throughout the physical body.

∞

THE SEVEN CENTERS OF SPIRITUAL POWER

The Chakras are an energetic system of Spiritual power or life force energy for our body. The health of our physical body is the manifestation of how well we manage our spiritual power and life force energy.

The Chakras assist in the running of our body, mind, and soul. If the life force of a chakra is not balanced, this could cause our physical, mental, or spiritual health to suffer. There are many chakras in the body; however, we will only concentrate now on the seven major chakras. They start from the base of the spine and move upward to the crown of the head, and they are positioned along the spinal cord.

The First Chakra – The Root Chakra
This chakra is located at the base or tail end of the spine. The first chakra is the foundation of the physical body. It stimulates vital forces throughout the body and assists in keeping us grounded to the earth. It influences our immune system, our basic instincts, impulses, endurance, and our fight or flight reactions. This chakra relates to family, culture, religion, social attitudes, and behaviors that were absorbed during childhood. Giving away our energy to the social world to think for us, to tell us about ourselves, and to live our lives for us, is a way to lose a lot of power in this chakra.

The organs associated with this chakra are muscles, bones, hip joints, spine, blood, and immune system. When spiritual or emotional issues like fear, mistrust, or dependency block the life force energy of this chakra, related physical problems are manifested in the body.

The Second Chakra – Sacral Chakra – Sexual Chakra
This chakra is located in the lower abdomen approximately two inches from the belly button. This chakra is the source of creativity and

inspiration. The organs associated with this chakra are the uterus, ovaries, vagina, cervix, penis, prostate, testes, large intestine, lower vertebrae, pelvis, appendix and bladder. This chakra represents our sexuality, creativity, finances, personal power, relationships, sensuality, and pleasure. So it is the place that deals with control issues, genitals, survival issues, and our relationship with people. This chakra is the place where we feel threatened, where we relate to love and friendship, and this is also the place that affects our bank account.

Money is energy that flows and manifests in the physical world according to the beliefs we choose to energize. Hence money is not in the bank account but it is in the lower back and hips. Chronic lower back pain is frequently triggered by financial stress. When we struggle with physical and emotional issues like sexual drive, money, relationships, and defining boundaries, related physical problems occur in the body.

The Third Chakra – Solar Plexus Chakra

The third Chakra is situated at the base of the ribcage. This Chakra enables us to pick up vibrations and essences from people places and things. It is the place of our sense of self-esteem. We lose enormous power here, and we often find ourselves covering this place with our hands when we feel uncomfortable. This chakra involves our personal power, self control, emotional issues, and issues of self-acceptance. It represents the development of our personality.

The organs associated with this chakra are the abdomen, upper intestine, liver, gall bladder, stomach, kidney, pancreas, spleen, adrenal system, and middle spine. Spiritual and emotional issues of self-confidence, self-respect, competition, addictions, aggression, and making decisions block the energy of the third chakra and create related physical problems in the body.

The Fourth Chakra – The Heart Chakra

This Chakra is situated in the center of the chest around the area of the heart. This chakra represents forgiveness, compassion, trust, balance, and ease in life. It is a place of the merging of the physical with the spiritual world. It also connects us with the plant, animal, mineral, and angelic kingdoms. The Heart chakra collects all of the data of our love experience, harmony, and happiness. It is the real power center of the body.

When the heart chakra is balanced and in harmony with the upper and lower chakras of the body, it allows for unconditional love, rejuvenation, and wellbeing in all areas of life.

Physical organs associated with this chakra are the heart, lungs, blood vessels, shoulders, ribs, diaphragm, and esophagus. Spiritual and emotional issues of anger, hostility, grief, and issues of forgiveness block the energy flow in this chakra and thus manifest related physical problems in the body.

The Fifth Chakra – The Throat Chakra

The fifth Chakra is situated at the base of the neck in the throat. This chakra influences communication, artistic expression, good judgment, wisdom, truthfulness, out-of-body experiences and clairaudience. It represents faith and higher communication. This is the chakra that influences your sense of choice, sense of will, and your capacity to know yourself.

Organs associated with this chakra are the thyroid, trachea, neck vertebrae, throat, mouth, teeth and gums. When spiritual and emotional issues of struggles with speaking, listening, waiting, or using our will arise, we lose energy in this chakra. When there is discomfort in this chakra, our hand will automatically go to the back of the neck.

The Sixth Chakra – The Third Eye Chakra

This chakra is situated in the middle of the forehead – linking the eyebrows. The third eye chakra influences our capacity to see with clarity including things of the future. It is the place of our psychic powers. This chakra represents our intuition, imagination, visualization, finely tuned awareness, and reasoning.

The organs associated with the sixth chakra are the brain, eyes, ears, nose and the pineal gland. This chakra is the center of reality, and we construct our beliefs and our attitudes here. If this chakra is balanced, we feel in control of our lives, we are confident in our own abilities, and we do not need to look to others to feel whole. This is the place of our power. When spiritual and emotional issues of mental clutter, morality, limiting rules and belief systems block the energy of this chakra, related physical problems occur.

The Seventh Chakra – The Crown Chakra

The seventh chakra is situated at the top of the head or crown area. The seventh chakra is the foundation of our spiritual body and links us to guidance from our Celestial Soul. It is our connection to our spiritual nature and our Divine Self.

This is the Grace bank account where we store the energy from our good deeds and our prayers accumulated from every lifetime on earth. The energy from this chakra allows spirituality to become a part of our physical life.

Physical organs influenced by this chakra are the cerebral cortex, central nervous system, cerebrum, the pineal and the pituitary glands, and all organs of your system. This center serves as the place of spiritual connection and in times of energy block, it will bring a wake-up call to the body in the form of illness or accidents.

∞

THE GIFT OF AWARENESS

The blocks in the chakras are created to stop the depletion of life force energy. The illness in the body may be healed but the blocks can last longer, and they may even be carried from lifetime to lifetime through the cell's memories. Being aware of the imbalances in the chakras and dysfunction in the body helps us to recognize where we are losing our energy. Every time we think and give emotions to our wounds, we are disempowering ourselves as we will lose energy from one of the chakras.

True healing requires us to pay attention to our wounds of the past, to forgive ourselves and others, and to have a sense of honor and integrity toward ourselves. For ages, we have become comfortable with storing data, keeping account, and suffering. We have become story-tellers of stressful stories and we project our stories outward as the world around us. We define our lives by our wounds, and our social climate celebrates our wounded stories of the past and the present. We believe that if we do not have a story of hurt to share, then we have nothing to converse about with each other. We love to tell our stories of pain, but we do not really face our pain. We consider pain to be our enemy, and we try to run away and escape from it. Pain is actually our guardian. It is our body talking to us and asking us to be in our truth.

Healing is not perfection. Healing is redefining ourselves and working through our challenges in truth and integrity as a day to day life journey. Instead of asking *why*, we change by asking the question *how*. The moment we ask why we remain stagnant and we deplete our energy. When we ask how, we will be shown the way and our life moves on. We can have a million thoughts a day, but if we choose not to believe them or to attach our emotions to them, we remain in peace.

We do not actually love others; we only love the concepts we have about them. We project our concepts on to the world and we compare. It is not possible to have the idea of a mistake unless we are comparing our ideas and concepts with the reality of the world outside. The concept of a mistake happens only in the mind story. As long as we hold on to a negative concept about someone, we will continue to project it on to everyone. This is how we create a discord in our reality. So if there is a discord in our reality on the outside, we need to go within and heal the concept inside us. When we learn to love ourselves truly, it will not be possible to project the concept that other people do not love us. What we give to ourselves, we will project on to the world outside.

We deplete our energy by attaching to our judgments about the world. Instead of healing ourselves, we start searching for that perfect person who would love and understand us and complete us in all of the ways that we could not. In our search, we demand that our parent, spouse, or children validate the caring, the love, the nurturing, the acceptance, and the respect that we are not giving ourselves. That is why we want them to behave according to our ideals and our concepts. We try to mould them to our whims and fancies, and we create discord in our relationships when they are not what we want them to be. We never get to truly know them or see them as they are as we constantly seek to see them only from our ideals. Hence, we lose the joy of knowing the true person in our lifetime.

Each person is a universe unto themselves. Each person can understand only their own story. No one can ever understand another person's story, and even if they do understand, it will only be from their perspective. Therefore, no one will be able to love or understand you the way that you want. Realizing this is a grand freedom. Realizing this we come to the understanding that the only person who can love and understand us the way we want is our own self. We are the ones we are seeking. The only true love affair is what we have with ourselves. The experience of love and understanding cannot come from anyone outside us; it can only come from within us. I cannot tell you truly that I love you, all I can say is "I love me more when I am with you" or "I love me more for having created you in my space."

We are one hundred percent responsible for our own happiness; no one has authority over our life as only we have the authority. By noticing the concepts and thoughts that we attach to, we realize that no one can frighten us – it is our own doing. The world is a projection of our thinking. So when we understand our thinking, we understand the world. When we are at peace within ourselves, the world is at peace. When we love ourselves, there is clarity in our mind and through clarity we can see that all is good. We are all absolutely safe, and there are no mistakes in the Universe.

∞

SPIRITUAL TOOLS
Using the Rose Tool to Clear the Chakras

Ground yourself to Mother Earth and connect with your heart. See yourself in the center of your head and visualize a rose. You can work with the colors of the chakra for the rose you create.

First chakra – red
Second chakra – orange
Third chakra – yellow
Fourth chakra – green/pink
Fifth chakra – blue
Sixth chakra – indigo
Seventh chakra – violet

Begin by sending a red rose to your First Chakra and ask it to collect up the energy of fear and every emotional and spiritual issue that does not support you at this time. When your rose has finished collecting the energy thank the rose and explode it.

Now in the same way you can create an orange rose for the second chakra and ask it to collect up the energy of fear and every emotional and spiritual issue that does not support you at this time. When your rose has finished collecting the energy thank the rose and explode it.

Create a yellow rose for the third chakra and ask it to collect up the energy of fear and every emotional and spiritual issue that does not support you at this time. When your rose has finished collecting the energy thank the rose and explode it.

For the fourth chakra create a pink rose and ask it to collect up the energy of fear and every emotional and spiritual issue that does not support you at this time. When your rose has finished collecting the energy thank the rose and explode it.

Send a blue rose for the fifth chakra and ask it to collect up the energy of fear and every emotional and spiritual issue that does not support you at this time. When your rose has finished collecting the energy thank the rose and explode it.

You can create an indigo rose for the sixth chakra and ask it to collect up the energy of fear and every emotional and spiritual issue that does not support you at this time. When your rose has finished collecting the energy thank the rose and explode it.

Now in the same way you can create a violet rose for the seventh chakra and ask it to collect up the energy of fear and every emotional and spiritual issue that does not support you at this time. When your rose has finished collecting the energy thank the rose and explode it.

Now connect with your Celestial Soul with gratitude and pure intention and ask to be balanced and healed. Your Celestial Soul sends you a golden ball of vibrant energy made of unconditional love and light. The ball is the size of a large orange. This golden ball will completely replenish each chakra with the golden energy of your Celestial Soul.

With your in-breath, see this energy ball of golden light slowly descend through your crown filling your entire being with a purple golden light.

See the golden ball travel down to your third eye chakra, merging and becoming a golden indigo light.

When you feel comfortable, allow the golden ball to travel to the throat chakra and see the blue golden light healing the throat chakra.

Now let the golden ball slide down to the heart chakra and notice the heart chakra fill with a golden green color. Allow for the feeling of comfort and joy to happen as your heart fills.

Allow the golden ball to move down to the solar plexus chakra, and see the chakra filled with yellow-gold light. Stay in the comfort of this feeling for some time.

Now allow the golden ball to move down to the sacral chakra, and see the chakra shimmering and shining like the orange gold evening sun.

When you are filled, allow the golden ball to travel to the root chakra, and see the root fill with a red gold light. Feel the joy and the comfort.

Now allow this golden ball to travel back up to your sacral chakra. Allow it to rest there and continue to fill your system with healing love and light.

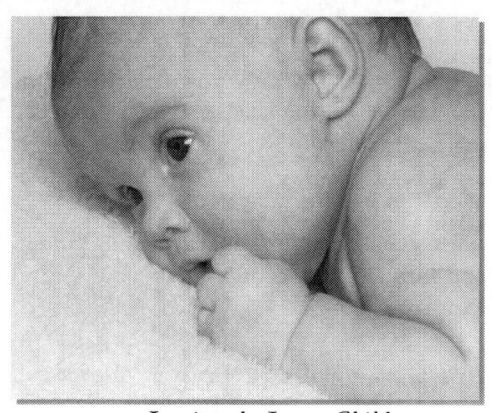

Loving the Inner Child

When we pay attention, we give ourselves the gift of knowing that we are responsible in creating our reality. We sabotage our life from the beliefs that we are not worthy, that we are not good enough, and that we do not deserve. Fear is the cause for our emotional reactions. It does not matter what name we give the fear; it can be anger, stress, jealousy, lust, greed, abuse, or anything. Emotional reactions such as this heavily deplete our life force energy. Love is the powerful transformer, and so it is important to learn to choose love.

Every emotional reaction to situations in life is the reaction of a wounded inner child, the child who lives within us in fear. All this little child wants is to be swept into your arms and be comforted, assured of safety and told how much it is loved.

At one time deep in meditation, I saw myself in my past as a little girl of 7 or 8 years old, I was extremely distressed and crying outside my home. I saw this kind lady come and sit near me, she spoke words of comfort and hugged me. I realized in my meditation that it was me myself as an adult who had visited me as a little girl. After this experience, for more than a year, my dreams were all about little children and babies. My soul revealed to me that my inner child needed a lot of comfort and love. This lead me into my powerful journey of healing my inner world and finding magic and miracles in the world outside. The following is a powerful meditation to heal the inner child.

Meditation

Sit in a chair with your back straight and your feet on the ground. Ground and center yourself, notice your breathing. Connect with your heart and smile, do the pranic breathing connecting with Father-Mother God. As you allow your breath to flow through your heart, visualize reaching out and gathering yourself in your arms as a little child. Place this little child lovingly on your lap and hug the little child. Tell this little child softly,

> "My beloved, I love you very much. I will not leave you. We are in this life journey together. This world is a safe place and we are evolving together. We are Divinely Protected and Guided."

As you are lovingly hugging this child and being in this meditative state, you will feel a warmth spreading throughout your body; there may even be goose bumps on your skin. A grand miraculous transformation takes place – for at this moment you are centered, your energy centers are healed, and the life force energy is entering your body and filling every cell of your body with health and vitality. Do this meditation as many times as you can. The more you do it, the more you will be able to love and comfort yourself.

When you love every aspect of yourself fully, you awaken to the truth of who you are. Loving the inner child, you bring in this miraculous transformation for your body, mind, and soul. This is a process of choosing love. You are powerful, you connect with your wholesome self, and you bring about the transformation. The conscious choice of loving the self is true living.

It is about living the truth of who you are. Living from your truth, you bring in more love, more joy, more fun, more laughter, more beauty, more harmony, and more peace into your life. Loving the Self and living from your truth is true enlightenment! It is awakening to self-realization!

Energy Tools

As we consciously choose to reconnect with our spiritual energy and ask for guidance, we begin to see our limiting beliefs and free ourselves from them. We connect with our Spirit and our Celestial Soul. We free ourselves from energetic imbalance and restore our energy to its naturally high vibration with which we can achieve physical, emotional, and psychological wellbeing.

Many energy techniques that can heal the chakras, release limiting beliefs, and rejuvenate our life force are available around us. Below are some of those energy healing techniques.

Energy healings that involve physical touch or activity of the body are: Reiki; Qigong; Tai Chi; Falun Dafa; Acupuncture; Acupressure; EFT; Magnified Healing; Quantum healing; and Mudras.

Energy Healings that involve the use of flowers, plants, or crystals are: Bach flower remedies; Aromatherapy; healing with flower essences; and healing with crystals and gemstones.

Energy healings that involve the use of sound and symbols are: Hemi-Sync therapy; Quantum K healing; Theta wave therapy; Sound healing music; crystal bowls; tuning forks; and sound tables.

Also there are many other energy healings such as rainbow

rays, color therapy, art therapy, music therapy, and dance therapy as well as different kinds of breathing techniques, pranic breathing, visualizations, and meditations.

You can choose to learn and practice any of the energy healings that resonate with you and give the grand gift of wellness and Inner Peace to yourself and this Planet.

Clearing Agreements – Releasing People – Managing Grief

Be aware of yourself in a much more conscious level. The following is a powerful spiritual tool to release people from your consciousness and also to take back your power. In doing this exercise you are also giving people their energy back. Many times we fill much of our space with other people's energies and tend to depend on them to complete us. We forget to live from the place of our power.

Connect with the heart. The heart is a place of transformation and hence, emotions like grief, sadness, and depression cannot persist there.

Intense negative emotions are due to people putting themselves into each others' space. Human emotions are carried by the opinions of the mind:

"I love you, you love me, I am like you, and you are like me… so I love you."

In this way, we attach so much emotion to our opinions. Human emotions of love that are attached only to opinions will dissipate overtime.

When a person's opinion is not exciting anymore, they decide that they are done with the relationship, and they take their energy with them. They rip off their energy from the other person's space:

"I am taking me back from you, or I may or may not give you back to you."

Energy loss such as this may happen due to death or separation. Absence of the energy called love from one's space creates great grief, sadness, and depression. In order to fill this absence of energy, people search for energy from the wrong places and bring more confusion into their lives. The only way the holes in your energy field can be healed is by you replacing it with You. Grief happens when we give away ourselves expecting validation to be returned. The reality of all relationships is:

"I love me more when I am with you. I love me for creating you in my space."

It is wise to empower oneself with the love and light of the Creator, to let go of other people's energies from our space, and to take back the energy we left in their space. This allows us to become our wholesome, powerful selves.

You can think of the person who is consistently on your mind, who may be irritating you, and whose energy you would like to remove from your space. This is not necessarily a bad energy – it is only that you would like to heal and be your wholesome self, and you would also allow the person to take back his or her energy and feel whole again. This is a profound gift that you can give to people by giving them back to themselves.

Ground yourself to Mother Earth and connect with your heart. See yourself in the center of your head. From the center of your head, see your view screen. Visualize a rose of any color and place the person inside the rose. See the rose change color as this is the color of that person's energy that is in your space.

Now visualize another rose next to the first one. This rose represents you – notice the color of this rose.

Now give the command to the other person's rose to collect up all of his or her energy from your rose. Now give the command to your rose to collect all of your energy from his or her rose.

When the roses have finished exchanging energy from each other, take a moment to thank the person. You can think of anything that you appreciate about her or him and offer gratitude. Now explode that person's rose and make it disappear. The person's energy will return back to him or her.

Now take your rose and fill it with the golden energy of your Celestial Soul and allow it to enter your body. The rose will replenish your body with life force energy wherever needed.

∞

11 RELATIONSHIPS

"Tell everyone you know, my happiness depends on me – so you're off the hook. And then demonstrate it. Be happy, no matter what they're doing. Practice feeling good, no matter what. And before you know it, you will not give anyone else responsibility for the way you feel – and then, you'll love them all. Because the only reason you don't love them, is because you're using them as your excuse to not feel good." ~Abraham-Hicks

∞

ALL RELATIONSHIPS BEGIN FROM LOVING THE SELF

To have harmonious relationships outside the self, one must first heal the relationship within the self. Relationship with oneself begins by loving and accepting oneself completely. We are responsible for our happiness absolutely. No one can make us happy or sad as it is our freewill to make ourselves happy or sad. We look at the world from our perception and we create our reality from the meaning we choose to give to life.

When we learn to love and accept ourselves completely, humility is born. Humility is emptying oneself of all of the stories of the past. Removing all of the labels of who or what we think we are. It is a most challenging journey and it is the journey to transformation. Without loving and accepting the self, one cannot understand humility. If we try to practice humility before loving and understanding the self, we will tend to live from the stories of woundedness, self pity, and lack of self esteem. Many times we give the meaning of humble to be weak.

Humility is not about weakness or lack of self esteem. Humility is power through emptying the self of past stories in order to allow the LOVE of the Creator to flow through. You cannot truly receive when you are full of the past stories of the *I* as the story of the *I* completely fills you and there is no space for the Creator anywhere.

"You are nothing but your Past. What are you? Just a collection of the past. Drop your past, and you are not. The ego is nothing but a collective name for your whole past; and when you don't live in the past, you start living egolessly. Then moment to moment you go on dying to the past, you go on renouncing the past, and each moment you are fresh, young, virgin. And in that virginity is God." ~Osho

Humility is the place of complete emptiness – emptiness to a sense of *I*. As long as there is an *I*, there is the control of the ego mind. The *I* likes to give but not to receive, it likes to keep memories, it likes to keep accounts, it summarizes and compares, and it thinks that it is all knowing. Only when we learn to drop the *I*, do we become the empty cup where the Divine Presence can fill us. We cannot receive if we are full of the *I*. We continue to give, to interact from the place of *I*, and we never know to receive. Receiving love, grace, and kindness from people around us and from the divine becomes very difficult when we do not empty the *I* in ourselves. The foundation for a true relationship is in giving and receiving as relationships must be balanced with giving and receiving. If there is no one to receive what you give, how will you be able to give it, how will you come to know what generosity is, and what love is. A true relationship is born from dropping the *I*, to let go of control, and to let go of the past and all of its stories of hurt and distress.

Only when we drop the stories of the past, we will become empty to receive, enjoy, and savor love. A relationship with the Creator or with anyone outside the self is fulfilled only when we have relaxed into the place of emptying, allowing, and accepting.

Relationships are based on true love, and true love is never an emotion. True love is a conscious connection with the Divine Presence. When we empty ourselves of all of the *I* stories and labels stored in our memories, we allow the love of God to pour into our beings. And when we are filled with the love of God, we return to True Love. The attributes of true love are explained in the *Bible:*

1 Corinthians chapter 13: If I speak in the tongues[e] of men or of angels, but do not have love, I am only a resounding gong or a clanging cymbal.
2 If I have the gift of prophecy and can fathom all mysteries and all knowledge, and if I have a faith that can move mountains, but do not have love, I am nothing.
3 If I give all I possess to the poor and give over my body to hardship that I may boast, but do not have love, I gain nothing.
4 Love is patient, love is kind. It does not envy, it does not boast, it is not proud.
5 It does not dishonor others, it is not self-seeking, it is not easily angered, it keeps no record of wrongs.
6 Love does not delight in evil but rejoices with the truth.
7 It always protects, always trusts, always hopes, always perseveres.
8 Love never fails.

Living life without true love is chaos and confusion. For when we do not allow the Divine Presence, the mind takes over and controls our every move with its fear stories. True living is building our relationship to God, our relationship to life, and how it serves others.

Every human relationship is made to nurture and take care of each other. Living from the mind in the busyness of the world we lose our connection to life and relationships. When we forget our connection, we starve psychically, emotionally, and spiritually. Life is so benevolent that it always opens a way for us to learn, to grow, and be inspired.

Our seeking for higher consciousness is a grand step toward healing and harmony. When we start to empty ourselves of our stories, it is a most profound healing work we do for ourselves.

∞

THE PATH OF TRANSFORMATION

Seeking higher consciousness and following the path of the mystic is a lonely road, and it cannot be reasoned out logically. Trying to follow the spiritual path in a busy, modern world is like living in a monastery and depriving oneself of the comfort zone of mental stories. The stories of the ego mind imprison us to the world of illusions – they are like the eclipse that hides the light of our spirit as we experience life as negative and dark.
Experiencing the death of the stories of the past is powerful. It feels like actual death. When we see people on their deathbeds, they look so happy as they are out of the constant decision making from the mind, and the constant stress of taking control. They are giving up the delusion of being in charge, they have decided to go with the experience of death, and they are in freedom, peace, and joy.

Saint John of the Cross, explains the journey of the soul from its bodily home to its union with God as "The Dark Night." The darkness here is the difficulties one faces because of detachment to the mind stories about the world. For some people, the dark night is triggered by external events that may be a horrendous experience of near death, betrayal, the loss of a loved one, loss of finances, loss of relationship, or isolation and so forth. This makes them seek for the level of faith in themselves that they never sought before.

In the death of the mind stories, the light of understanding is born, and this light is the light of true living. You live from the place of the true you because all of your defenses are gone. You are not a somebody anymore and you become a nobody – a person with no labels, completely vulnerable, completely at the mercy of Divine Love, and completely in the place of trust. The light of understanding shows you the true you, it shows you your vastness, and your connection with the All. You cannot be confined to a name, a role, or a form anymore.

When we die, if we look back to our life, it may feel like a dream. We are the dreamers, and we are the creators of our reality. The meaning for everything in life is the meaning we give it. We are not the dream, but we are the dream makers. Transformation is waking up from the dream and understanding ourselves as the consciousness that dreamed up the person. When we wake up and understand ourselves as consciousness, it is possible for us to create ourselves anew. Every creation we have been doing in the physical such as our jobs, our finances, our relationships, and everything, will be created anew with consciousness. It will not be a struggle as it will just flow with effortless ease.

∞

REASONING WITH LIFE

We are so possessed by our mind stories that we think that we have to think our way to live. Yet if we notice our breath and if we place our hand on our heart and notice our heart beat, we know that we are not doing the breathing or making the heart to beat. We are being breathed, we are being lived, and we are being moved every moment. There is absolutely nothing we can do to make our heart beat or make it stop beating. There is nothing for us to know, we do not need to pretend to know anything, and we live in absolute safety.

Looking at the night sky when we see the millions of stars, there is an awareness of something so deep and so powerful that holds them all in place. Meditation with the outer sky aligns us with our inner sky – our consciousness. We are made aware of the truth of who we are.

We have a tendency to want a logical reason for everything in life. We want everything to be explained from the place of blame or from the place of deservedness. Trials and pain are considered to be bad by logic and arguments with life start to block the light of Spirit. Addicted to reasoning, we suffer in search of answers. Life; however, is much grander than logic.

The road to healing becomes long and tedious when we live from the place of reasoning with life. There are no logical reasons to explain life situations. Our minds can only see the picture in front of us; therefore, there is no understanding of the greater tapestry of life. Every situation in life is divinely orchestrated and every situation lays the ground work to prepare us for something in the future.

Freewill is our gift. We can to choose to relate to life situations by exercising our freewill. We can either choose to be still and allow the Divine Presence to flow through us and heal us, or we can choose to suffer from our mind stories and die to life.

When we choose to look at life through the lens of reasoning, we continue to struggle. We think that if we find a reason we can be healed, we can get back our lost jobs, or our lost relationships. But life does not work that way. Many therapies seek to find a reason, but there is no particular reason for anything in life.

Doctors are also now finding that common medications do not work the same way for everyone as each individual is unique. Each human is an amazing collection of hundreds of life experiences and hundreds of decisions made at every point throughout life. Hence, to give one reason for any situation is insufficient.

∞

HEALING

Healing is about transforming our relationship to life, and it is about understanding our values and purpose in life. Healing is a mystical experience and the journey cannot be made from the mind. Healing is a journey and not a destination. We never stop healing as every moment life brings us newer situations to deal with, to grow from, and to gather wisdom from. Choosing to live from the place of gratitude is true devotion to the Divine. There is absolutely no purpose in life other than the purpose to live in love and trust. Every purpose of life that the mind can come up with is just a thought for survival. You cannot add or delete anything in life to achieve success, to feel good, or to give more value. Life has already provided all these things for you in the here and now and you only need to open your eyes to see these gifts.

Everything in life is divinely orchestrated. This moment, this day, and this hour is a precious gift – it will never come again. Live from the place of gratitude and learn to see the gifts of life. Take every person in your life, exaggerate their goodness, and notice the gifts they bring to your life at this time. Your gratitude to life becomes a living prayer. Bring in excitement with gratitude.

Celebrate love, celebrate life, surrender the mind stories, and drop the illusion of control. Let life live you and allow the Divine Presence to walk your life. When you understand that life lives you all of the time, you do not need destinations or goals to achieve because whatever life brings is for your greater growth and wisdom. It is wise to live from the place of excited anticipation of the next moment like a little child the eve before Christmas.

Write the words: "Something Magical is about to Happen," in beautiful big letters. Post it to your fridge, your work table, your bathroom mirror, and read it every day. Expect magic and miracles, drop all of your mind stories and become a little child waiting in excited anticipation. Life loves you greatly, you are a beloved child of the Universe, and when you are in the place of excited anticipation, the Universe brings magic and miracles into your life.

> "Whatever the present moment contains, accept it as if you had chosen it.... this will miraculously transform your whole life." ~Eckhart Tolle

About 10 years ago, we migrated to the USA as a family. The first year of life was tough for we had to start all over again in a new country. It was a Valentine's Day week and I went to Wal-Mart to purchase my groceries. I was so excited to see all of the beautiful flowers and balloons displayed for Valentine's Day as soon as I entered the store. I wanted so much to buy a bunch of flowers for myself, but noticing the price I knew that I could not afford them. Money was tight and we had to budget it for our essential needs. So I just decided to stand near the flowers and gaze at them while giving thanks. My husband told me to take my own time and enjoy looking at the flowers. I touched and held each bouquet with immense love and joy from my heart, and I gave thanks that the flowers were there in my life at that very moment for me to enjoy. I stood there and thanked Mother Earth for her graciousness in providing such beauty and joy for All. I then went home so happy and filled with joy.

On this same day, it so happened that in the evening two American friends wanted to visit with us. I made a nice East Indian dinner for them. When my friends came and knocked on my door, I opened it and found them standing with two huge bouquets of flowers. One was a bouquet of huge red roses, and the other was a variety of lilies that I have never seen in my life! I was so thrilled and rejoiced in the miracle of life, and I hugged and thanked my friends for their thoughtfulness. I placed my hands on my heart and thanked the Divine for this wondrous love. When we align ourselves and our existence with gratitude and joy, every detail of our life is filled with blessing.

FINDING ALIGNMENT WITH EXISTENCE IS THE GOAL OF LIFE

Consciousness expresses itself as a human, and when the human chooses to be awake, consciousness expresses itself as unconditional love. Unconditional love has no beginning and no ending, and it is beyond likes and dislikes. Relating to life is an ongoing phenomenon. Consciousness chooses to relate to people, places, and situations by giving, receiving, allowing, accepting, growing, and gathering wisdom. Choosing to relate to life from the mind stories creates confusion. Seeking union with the Divine and living life from the place of alignment, makes relationships meaningful.

Very often relationships fail because we relate to people and things from the concepts of our mind. There is so much of staleness and inflexibility in concepts. We try to compare our relationship to the fantasy or projection of our minds, and in the comparison, the world outside seems imperfect.

We are eternal beings of infinite expansion, our consciousness continues to expand, and we change continuously. A relationship that does not accommodate change will soon become stale. Conditions and inflexibility on partnership or relationships cannot work. When a relationship is related from a mind story of how it should be, we will never be able to see how the relationship truly is.

Flexibility to accommodate growth and change is the main foundation for successful relationships. Consciousness and expression are ever expanding, deepening, and the individual matures and becomes wiser. In a partnership when each individual values truth with an open mind and accepts the expansion and change of each other, the relationship will be a success.

The many years of relationship does not matter as all that matters is the growth in wisdom in a relationship. Relationships should become anew every moment. A relationship maintained by law, habit, or social consciousness, is a dead one.

The only way to keep a relationship alive is in searching for alignment with existence – the search to become alive – the search to live in union with the Divine. It is not in the search for mate, money, power, position or material things. In the search for alignment with existence, everything else in life is satisfied automatically. Love is the grandest tool of transformation. Love brings home the truth that there is no separation, and when we get out of the game of separation, our relationships become grand, magical, and respectful.

In truth every relationship in life whether it is with husband, wife, children, friends, neighbors, strangers, plants, animals, nature, or with creative expressions like drawing, painting, singing, music, dancing, and cooking is always a search for synchronicity with the Divine Presence. The formless Presence of the Divine enables all things to exist; it holds and nourishes all things within itself. Our relating to the things of existence with joy and gratitude is our dance with the Divine.

It is important to remember that all things that exist are equal as they are made of the same material. No one who has ever been born or will be born is greater or lesser than you. The only difference is how they choose to exercise their freewill with situations in life. Our job on the planet is not about making money, or working with people, or impressing those around us, or having security, or getting respect. Our job is to seek and find alignment with our source through relating with the things in existence. Things in existence are already in order even before they exist and there is no need to put anything in order. There is no one to rescue, nothing to teach, no one to be, and nowhere to go. Living without mental argument with existence is the grandest devotion to the Divine.

When we understand that we are one with existence, we stop searching for perfection. We stop comparing, we stop judging, and we stop arguing. For whatever we want at this moment is what we have with us at this moment. It is nothing more, and it is nothing less. Living in alignment with existence is living in total freedom and having our needs fulfilled all of the time. There is no possibility for anything in life to be against us – not even our ego. Hence, aligning with our Divine Presence is the first step toward any relationship.

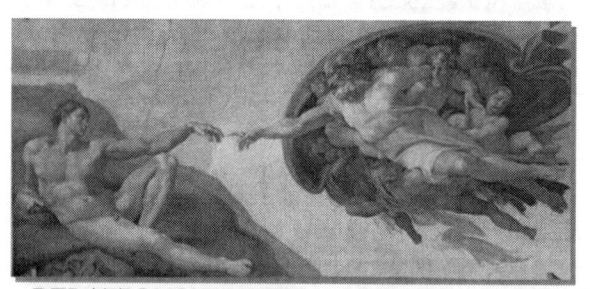

∞

RELATIONSHIP WITH THE BODY TEMPLE

"Bodies don't think, care, or have any problem with themselves. They never beat themselves up or shame themselves. They simply try to keep themselves balanced and healthy. They're entirely efficient, intelligent, kind, and resourceful. Where there's no thought, there's no problem. It is the story that we believe – prior to doing inquiry – that leaves us confused." ~Byron Katie

When we enter this Planet we bring with us this beautiful tool of creation – the human body. The body is a magnificent, mysterious being of immense wisdom. Connecting with the body's wisdom brings greater healing in all levels of consciousness. The body holds the consciousness of all levels – physical, mental, emotional, spiritual, psychic and cosmic. Unfortunately, many of us think that we are the body and so we never take time to connect with it. We are not this body; however, the body is a magnificent tool that helps us to expand our consciousness.

Connecting with the body intelligence can happen only when there is emotional comfort. The emotional comfort helps the body to secrete its chemicals, juices, enzymes and hormones in a balance from its exotic pharmacy. This helps to strengthen the immune system and maintains physical wellbeing. In aligning with our Divine Presence, we bring emotional comfort into our lives.

The body dutifully gives feedback of the effects of thoughts and emotions. When we feed our body thoughts of joy and laughter, the body laughs and feels comfortable. But when we feed the body with thoughts of pain that happened yesterday, a few days ago, or 20 years ago, the body cries, becomes anxious, and goes into fear. The body does not know that this is only a thought, and it also does not know that this situation is not happening right now. Thus it reacts by secreting hormones and chemicals to balance the anxiety and worry. If we are feeding more of these thoughts each day, then the body reacts by secreting more of the anxiety hormones and this brings in more pain and disease. Pain and disease are messages from the body, and if we awaken and listen, we can change the situation.

The body loves it when you trust its intelligence and consciously connect with it. The body is a beautiful tool. You can program your body to wake you up at a certain time and after you sleep all night, you surprisingly wake up exactly at that time. The body is a beautiful pharmacist. It produces amazing medicines to heal and balance itself. It is magical to see the rejuvenation when we connect with our bodies. The body works well with our awareness. Awareness is our sacred Presence, and when we bring awareness to the body, we create wellbeing and peace in our bodies.

With this principle in mind, many physicians have cured their patients with the placebo effect. A placebo is a totally inactive substance typically used for experiment. When the patients have belief in their doctors, the doctors give them a sugar pill (a placebo) and say that it is a powerful medicine to heal their sickness. Miraculous healings have happened without any actual medical treatment but just by the belief of the patient. The patient's belief in the power of the medication triggered the body to heal.

The body is an intelligent being and it listens to our thoughts and emotions, it responds to awareness, and when we consciously connect with the body, our body comes alive with health, youth, and vitality.

∞

Kit Alderson

THE SACRED CONNECTION TO FOOD

Every particle of food that we eat becomes our cells and tissues. When we do not respect the food we eat, we also do not respect our bodies. Our bodies secrete powerful juices such as the saliva, the liver and bile juices. Our bodies have many enzymes to digest our food and balance our entire system. We need to listen to our body and eat food only when we are hungry. While we eat, our thoughts should be about the food. This will help the body to secrete the right amount of digestive juices and balance itself.

When we eat food mindlessly and are concentrating on our

worries, watching the television, or talking about depressing things with our friends, we are actually eating our sorrows and worries and they go into the body and react in the body as disease. Instead of secreting digestive juices, because we give our awareness to worries, the body secretes hormones to bring down the anxiety felt by the worry thoughts. Worry and anxiety are the main cause of producing acid in our body. As the nature of our body is alkaline, the body then has to work hard to make its inner atmosphere shift from acidic to alkaline.

If we take time to sit down at every meal and look at our food consciously, we will know that every grain of rice, wheat, corn, animal, or plant has willingly given its life for our bodies to live. What an amazing sacrifice this is! Realizing this is enough to make us be in the place of immense Gratitude for all of these beautiful beings around us.

Our bodies are sacred temples where the Divine resides. If we do not realize this and continue to feed our bodies with things that are not in harmony with it, then we end up with physical, mental, and emotional problems. Every addiction is due to mindlessness. When we refuse to be in the place of happiness and continue to stress ourselves with mind stories, the body is depleted of happy hormones. The nature of the body is to be happy. In order to balance itself, it tries to trigger the happy hormones by making us addicted to things that are not natural for us. We get addicted to sex, alcohol, drugs, shopping, sugar and so forth because we refuse to keep our mind and body at peace.

Humans are powerful beings born with the gifts of love, compassion, kindness, gentleness, intuition, and the power to heal themselves. Unless we consciously connect with ourselves, all these gifts that we have brought with us will never be revealed.

Our bodies have great intelligence. If we take the time to respect our body and listen to our body, we will evolve our grand gifts. Taking the time to lovingly touch and prepare our food is very important. The love and conscious connection we have with our food adds a miraculous spice to the food. The food becomes enriched with healthy and happy energy. The food tastes good.

When we sit down and eat our food consciously tasting and loving each bite, we are adding immense healing energy, we will never over eat or under eat, and we will never put things into our body that do not resonate with it. Eating mindfully, we will never get addicted in anyway. When we eat consciously, we allow all of the senses of the body (smell, taste, touch, hearing, seeing) to take part in the awesome creation of the experience of eating food. It becomes a Grand Experience – an experience that creates contentment for the body and mind.

People get out of diseases, lose unwanted weight, even get out of addiction when they sincerely take the time to respect themselves, their food, and consciously savor the experience of eating food. It is very satisfying when you eat silently by totally concentrating on every mouthful and affirming in your mind:

"I enjoy every particle of food I eat. I love every cell of my body."

There is enormous healing for body, mind, and spirit through this exercise.

∞

SACRED HUMAN CONNECTIONS

The last frontier of humanity is not the evolution of technology, but it is the evolution into Higher Consciousness. The projected world outside is the mirror image of the world inside. Every relationship becomes a tool for the evolvement of Higher Consciousness.

To become fully conscious of the true self, we need to understand that every single human being that comes into our space is a true reflection of us. If the person shows beauty, grace and wisdom, they are truly reflecting us, if they show greed, selfishness, or cruelty; they are also truly reflecting us. We live our lives denying our dark side. One of the most important spiritual practices is to acknowledge our dark side and understand that a person with dark qualities comes into our lives in order for us to bring this quality into the light. The moment we acknowledge and forgive the dark side in us, and willingly embrace both the light and dark sides of ourselves, we come to a better understanding of the Universal consciousness, and we begin to heal ourselves and our relationships.

Healing ourselves can happen only by aligning ourselves with our Divine Presence. The more we align ourselves, the more we will love and be in joy with ourselves. We will start enjoying our own company because our life will no longer be mind-ridden as it will be from the place of devotion to the Divine. Life becomes an overflowing joy for no reason, joy becomes our true nature, and we do not need to depend on anyone to bring us joy or comfort. We become a well spring of joy, and our joy is so infectious that it embraces all life in unconditional love.

Aligning with Divinity every day helps us to be aware of the mind stories and to drop them. Letting go the mind stories and letting go of searching for reasons, we come into our freedom from suffering. Duality of the world is not the suffering, but the mind stories about the duality is the cause of suffering.

Every human relationship is also a creation from our consciousness. As souls we choose our parents and families to be born into and as we start growing up, our consciousness chooses to bring people into our lives for us to relate, interact and grow with. When we are living from the mind story, we start judging, comparing, competing, blaming, and finally suffering with our relationships.

According to the words of Rumi:

"The minute I heard my first love story, I started looking for you, not knowing how blind that was. Lovers don't finally meet somewhere. They're in each other all along."

People do not come into our lives by chance or by accident. From our deep consciousness we create them in our life. We call unto their souls to come and play with us. When we are in alignment with our Divine Presence, we relate to people with gratitude and respect. Our joy and unconditional love overflows and helps our partners and us to grow in wisdom and to expand in consciousness.

Every human is unique. Every person lives in his or her own mind created world, and every person has his or her own ideas, thoughts, and concepts. Every human relationship is sacred because every relationship triggers a conflict with the mind stories. You are not even aware of your mind stories until someone comes along to challenge them. If you are living attached to your mind stories, much conflict and confusion will be created. But when you choose to align with your Divine Presence, you will be lead to drop your mind stories through the light of understanding. You will then be your own savior and you will not hold people responsible for your happiness. You will be aware that the sacredness of every human relationship is to help you to grow in wisdom and understanding.

∞

PARENTING WISDOM

Parenting wisdom is natural and every parent who is awake and aligned with existence becomes a successful parent. If one is not awake, one needs to depend for parenting wisdom from books, society, and education. When a child is born, a parent is also born. We are given the special tools and wisdom to nurture and care for our children. It is a grand gift of existence that is not available in books, society, or education. Books, society, and education are experiences of other people and can therefore only offer so much. However, aligning with the Divine Presence of our inner being, brings strength, wisdom and patience in bringing up children.

Every human parent strives to provide the best for their children. Parents like to see their child grow into a happy, healthy individual. But when one is attached to mind stories, parenting takes a different path. It brings a lot of pain when things go wrong. For parents think that they know what is best for their children. They have read all the books, discussed with their friends, doctors, and educators about parenting.

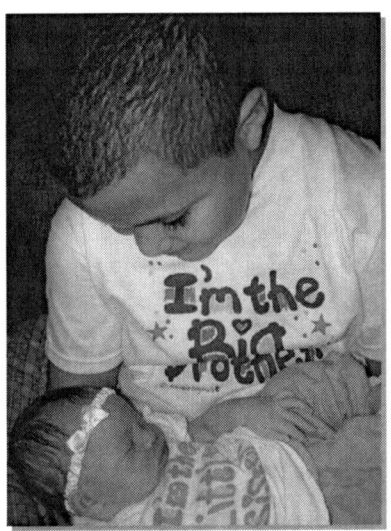

The first and foremost thing in parenting is aligning with the Divine Presence. Though we may have given our children their physical bodies, they are not the physical bodies. They are beautiful souls that are expressing through their bodies. When we connect with our Divine Presence, we understand soul connection, and we learn to see and connect with our children from our inner being.

When parenting is done from the mind, children are looked down upon as little people who do not know anything. Well-intentioned parents, teachers, and gurus try to impose their beliefs, ideas, fears, rules and laws on the children. The result produces fear. When there is fear, there is no place for love. It has become a collective learned human behavior to always be behind the children telling them what they should and should not do, and also to believe that punishment was for the child's good. This created much fear in the child, and fear made the child to break the laws. By creating laws and fear, we are teaching them to cheat and lie. We go on infecting children with ideas that have not even proved valid in our own lives. Many things we ask our children to do might not have been acceptable to us when we were in their age.

By forcing our children, we do not allow them to be authentic. They fear that they would hurt us if they are true, and they feel hurt when they are not true to themselves. Living from mind stories, we forget that we only gave a part of our physical bodies to our children and that the Spirit that activates the body comes only from the Creator. Children were never our possessions in the first place, and in this planet we are only their guardians.

When we realize this truth, we will also come into the understanding that we really do not know what is right or what is wrong for our children. They were brought into this world by the Creator through us, and the one that brought them into this world knows them more than we do.

Aligning ourselves to existence and allowing Divine Presence to flow through us, brings enormous wisdom in practicing the art of Parenting. The best and most effective way of parenting, is to serve as an example and not to impose our will.

Children need privacy and freedom. They are individual, unique souls who need to be respected and allowed to be themselves. They are not here to fulfill somebody's ideas. Their future is open and supported by a loving Creator. A wise parent is one who is there to give support, courage, and confidence to the child without harassing the child to live up to his or her expectations.

A wise parent understands that every human is beautifully programmed by the wisdom of the Creator, that there are no accidents, and that everything goes according to the program.

The best gift a parent can give the child is allowing and accepting the child to be his or her natural self wherever it leads to. Magic and miracles get created by this acceptance, and the gifts the child has brought to this planet are revealed.

∞

MINDFULNESS IN HUGGING ANOTHER BEING

Mindful hugging is a grand physical experience to relate to. Hugging is one of the greatest joys of being a human being. When we hug another human, an animal, or a tree with total awareness, our hearts connect and bring immense healing and happiness.

Our hands are the extensions of our hearts and when we embrace with our hands, we accommodate the entirety of another being into our hearts. It is simply thrilling to watch the hands; our hands bless us every day, and our hands take care of us. They feed us, they dress us, they comb our hair, brush our teeth, and they make things for us. But best of all they help us to hug another human being.

   Hugging mindfully brings us to the awareness that each being is sacred. Through hugging, we bring their Divine essence into the sacred place of our hearts. Our conscious breath enables us to feel from our hearts while breathing in and breathing out the sacred Presence of another. This brings the realization of the gift of this Present moment, the gift of togetherness, and the gift of the silent support we give to each other in this Planet of Beauty.

   Every conscious hug brings one to the Present moment, a moment that makes us aware to be mindful, a moment that shows us the sacred in every life, a moment that shows us the ease and grace of life beyond language, and a moment that creates healing, reconciliation, and conscious alignment with existence. It also brings with it an opportunity to bless another being from our hearts. The blessing can be silent or in language acknowledging the preciousness of the other being. Conscious hugging brings a powerful connection that can never be destroyed. A connection that stays sacred in our hearts long after the physical form has dissolved.

   Let us choose to bring this sacred connection into our lives. Let us choose to hug every being with sacred love from our heart center. Let us choose to give this gift to ourselves and to the Planet.

∞

Rock Crystal Shiva Lingam with Shiva Head.
Funan pre-Khmer culture in Cambodia, circa 8th century AD

SACRED SEXUALITY

Everything on the planet exists because of the constant movement of the Creative energies; everything in existence is energy. During this time of awakening on the Planet, it is imperative to understand the play of energies in our life. In every aspect of life, when energy is focused and directed wisely in union with divinity, it brings harmony and peace.

The Divine Presence that envelops you and all creation is charged with immense wellbeing. If it is your choice to empower yourself and expand your consciousness, the Universe is ever willing to support you in infinite ways. Emotions arise due to individual perceptions of reality; emotions can be handled only from the place of responsibility.

Sexual energy is the greatest challenge to our emotional balance. When we learn to love and communicate with our body with confidence, we will find greater fulfillment and meaning in life.

You are born as a beautiful sexual being; sexuality is your grandest creative energy, and sexuality is also your identity in this physical reality. Your beliefs about yourself and your self-worth condition your sexuality. Even though the media markets an extremely underrated version of sex, the truth about sexual energy is that it is a powerful creative energy capable of building an abundance of health, wealth, and happiness on the Planet.

Although the mind may suggest that sexual energy is due to physical attraction or social status, the deeper truth about sexual energy is that it exists beyond time and space. Its interest is to promote growth and transformation on the Planet. We are usually unaware of this.

Our interests and impulses that arise from within for our evolvement, propel us to meet a future mate or partner whose energy will help us to work on our issues to promote our personal growth and transformation. When the intimacy of sexual union is with openness and good intentions, the energy created between the partners is powerful enough to resolve these issues.

When we consciously value our body, trust our sexual nature, and live from the place of gratitude and self-worth, our energy will attract a like-minded partner. The combined energies of the partners can work wonders to enhance love, trust, respect, gratitude, and appreciation, which opens the great pathway into the world of spiritual awareness. Sex from the place of spiritual awareness brings immense joy, fun, laughter, healing, wellbeing, and emotional and physical pleasure. It leads one into a deeper connection with the energies of creation.

Sex is sacred and wonderful, and it has to be operated from the place of conscious awareness with respect for oneself as well as the society's moral values. Our genitals are sacred for they anchor the powerful creative energies of the universe. In the 1930s, Wilhelm Reich, an Austrian psychoanalyst, found that the orgasmic energy released during the sexual act was powerful enough to heal the physical body, the psychic health, and also the spiritual aspect of a person.

The orgasmic energy excites every cell of the body, and the mind releases its hold on the body. For a little while, we are in the place of no time, no space, freely floating, and enriching our Spirit with an abundance of life-force energy. When the Spirit is powerful, the body and mind become strong, and the connection with Spirit also is strengthened.

People who do not have sex for a long time can go into problems in their physical body. Our body is created holy and our genitals are an essential part of our body. We are born with our genitals; we cannot avoid them. Stimulating the physical body is essential for wellbeing. Many people also have a question about self-pleasuring the body; it is wise to listen to the body and its needs and love the body completely. Sexual release is a part of the body's vital function like breathing or circulation. And all vital functions help to maintain health and wellbeing.

When sexual expression accompanies love and trust, it brings immense health, a sense of wholeness, and a closer connection with the Divine. Although the sexual act involves physical connection of the genitals, the grander connection is the merging of the energy fields of the two partners. The energy body activates the energy centers (chakras) and stirs the body's glands to produce amazingly happy hormones capable of healing, rejuvenating, and altering the body chemistry.

Since sexual energy awakens the chakras, it releases all the buried feelings of many lifetimes. It opens one to face their deeper feelings and fears, and it allows one to work through them. It is for a very good reason that we meet a particular partner in our life as through our meeting, we are helped to work with our difficulties, and to create healing for our body, mind, and spirit.

Sacred sexual expression is a very clear communication with the Creator's energy. It is very important how we use our sexual energy. If the sacredness of sexuality is forgotten, or if we are using it to manipulate another person, then it is a misuse of the sacred energy, and it will create chaos. Any kind of misattribution of this sacred energy creates confusion beyond the human mind.

When sex gets perverted and is used to control, to devalue a person, or sex is used with vulnerable beings like animals or children, the sexual energy vibrates in the lowest of consciousness that allows and attracts negative vibrations of darkness to enter and take possession of the human body through the chakras. This is an invisible disease. With the fall of consciousness and lack of self-love, many people have allowed it to happen. Sex has been devalued and further perverted by religion, the acts of society, and modern media. Sexual energy is very powerful and due to its misuse, our Planet is in distress. The real intention behind every sexual perversion is power and possession. For thousands of years, men, women, and children have been treated as sexual objects by perverted beings filled with dark negative vibrational attachments. From ancient times and forward, there are individuals who use sexual abuse in rituals to gain personal power by offering the life force energy to these dark forces. Here again it may seem like a victim-villain game but these are unconscious agreements made because of a lack of self love and forgetting our connection with the divine. Every human has the power to wake up and cancel these agreements. Every human parent is responsible to teach their child to value their physical body and to love themselves. This is vital for us at this time in order to stop the game of the abuser and the abused. It is possible, and we have the power to do it.

When you do not value your body or your genitals and when you lack self-love, you will have no value for sexuality. This can allow dark negative vibrational attachments to form over that which you do not love. Today's society is riddled by boundary confusions of multiple sexual relationships where sex is further devalued by an attraction to pornography because of people's lack of self-love and self esteem. Since sex involves the exchange of energies, it is important to be acutely aware that we share and take on the energy, either negative or positive, of every person that we connect sexually with.

It is very important to commit to a relationship, whether it be same-sex or opposite-sex, with feelings of appreciation, love, and trust for yourself and for your partner. When you treat sex with sacredness, it will bring to you immense power and vitality for your body and mind. It will open your magical psychic connection with your Spirit body, heal and enhance your DNA, and bring you amazing wisdom of the cosmos. This is the Tantra of Sacred Sexuality. Tantra is a practice of conscious connection with one's divinity.

In India, the power of sacred sexuality is depicted in Shiva temples as the Shivalingam; it is the union of male and female creative powers, which is a grand generative power of nature. It is the responsibility of every human being to experience their sexuality with sanctity.

∞

RELATIONSHIP WITH WORK

The things we do with our body-mind are our creations in this physical realm. We lived before we came into this body and we took this human body at this time so that we may satisfy our Divine longing to do things in the physical. The body comes and goes but who we are is an eternal spark of the Creator that can never be damaged or destroyed. Hence, connecting to our Source is the best way to relate with all of the things we do in the physical.

We are great Spirit beings who come to live for a short time in a human body on this beautiful Planet. This is our opportunity to anchor our Divine qualities of love, kindness, compassion, forgiveness, patience, generosity, and gratitude on the Planet.

The moment we enter the planet in a physical body, we absolutely forget our Spirit selves and create a new chapter called *life on Planet Earth*. Our new body-minds start to develop, and the body-mind does not remember. But the heart that carries Divinity in its sacred sanctuary does remember and knows everything.

Practicing the art of awareness, aligning with existence, and bringing conscious awareness into every walk of life helps us to connect with our hearts and helps us to remember our mission here on Planet Earth.

We have been given this body-mind to work and to serve others, this Planet and ourselves. Are we conscious of our work at this moment? Every act of work whether cooking, cleaning, washing dishes, doing the laundry, taking care of children, teaching, working in an office, selling products, working on a computer, writing a book, talking to people, construction work, serving, tending, farming, or gardening is a profound gift we give ourselves and this planet. Our work is sacred, and when it is done with joy and an attitude of gratitude, we grow in wisdom and expand our consciousness.

When we bring our conscious awareness to the work we do, we are merging the Divine qualities of Spirit with matter, and we are building Heaven on Earth. No work is insignificant. All work we do with our body-mind is a miracle and it is a beautiful gift. When we become aware of the perfection of every moment, we do not need anyone else to appreciate us for what we do, and we can never see our work as being low or high in value. We realize that the place, time, the body-mind, the people around us, and the work we do have all been Divinely orchestrated.

It has become a human sickness to believe that we work hard for others. The belief that we work hard for a boss, for an institution, or for a country makes our work a drudgery. Another belief that work is for earning money makes people addicted to work. The Greater truth is that we work for ourselves as every act of work is an opportunity to expand our consciousness and grow in wisdom. It is an opportunity for us to show kindness to our fellow beings, and it is a grand experience! When we realize this we will always respect the work we do, our work will never be about harming or destroying, and our work will be about building and uplifting. Being grateful every moment and holding the joy of doing work in a physical body, uplifts our Spirit and our work then becomes true worship. Let us choose to respect ourselves and the work we do every day.

∞
RELATING TO TIME AND MONEY

All of existence is made from the material of consciousness-source-God. There is no separation, everything is equal, and everything in existence is made of the same material. Our relationship to things of existence depends on our growth in consciousness.

Time and money are also the grand creations of consciousness. But separating time and money as power and attaching to it is the story of the mind. Believing our mind stories, we attach ourselves to our physical world intensely. We have hypnotized ourselves into believing that being busy all of the time is purposeful and noble. The busier we are, the more important we feel about ourselves. The material world is only one part of our reality, but we have started to define others and ourselves by what we produce. We stress ourselves out with achievements, deadlines, and productions. In a world of overwork, our hearts harden, and illness and pain become our companions.

We are multidimensional beings who also live in the invisible and spiritual dimensions. Just by watching our thoughts, we know that there is a being who watches the thoughts. Just by watching the body perform its actions, we know that there is a being who works the body. Our dreamtime feels so real that it makes us wonder if we were in another place at another time. If we travel to space in a rocket we come to know that the sun never sets nor does it rise, and we also understand that the directions of north, south, east, or west are just a concept in a map. We are much more than who we think we are, and existence is much grander.

Every religion talks about a day of rest, a day to make sacred; a Sunday for Christians, a Saturday for Jews, and a Friday for Muslims and Hindus. Living in our minds, we believe that it is one day of the week where we do things other than our regular work. Reserving a sacred day is a practice to move into state of rest, renewal, and conscious connection to the Divine. It is a spiritual practice to realign with our birthright to inner peace. When we take time to anchor our Spiritual Energy, it balances our life. We become our wholesome selves, and we come into our power.

Consciously choosing to organize our time to connect with our Divine Presence is a wise way to relate to our time and money. Our sacred connection can be a moment, a day, a week, or a month. It can be taking in a deep conscious breath anytime during the day, it may be meditation, it may be connecting with nature, sitting in stillness, or even a mental act of counting our blessings.

At the deepest level we are pure consciousness beyond form and content. We are made of unconditional love. The moment we connect and align with our Divine Presence, it embraces everything within and around us. Mysteriously, our body feels embraced, healed, and comforted by this love, and every situation dealing with time, money, or relationships on the outside is also set right. This is our wholesome power as every creation happens from here and abundance in life flows from here.

Choosing to live in joy and gratitude, taking time to laugh more, to play more, and to choose to celebrate every aspect of life, is a successful way to relate to time and to manifest abundance in life.

∞

SACRED BREATH

You are LIFE. You come to know that you are life only when you are aware of your breath. Many times we go through the busyness of our human situations without giving another thought to our breath. But we all know that we are now here only because of the breath – that if the breath is taken away then we do not physically exist on the Planet anymore.

All religious, spiritual, meditative, and therapeutic practices talk about the breath as the way to health, wellbeing, self-discovery, and self-transformation.

Placing one's awareness on the breath is a powerful way to connect with our body and with our inner world. The ego-mind is constantly busy keeping us rooted either in the past negative happenings or in worry about the future. Placing awareness on the breath is the only way to be released from this sickness of the mind.

One conscious breath can overpower the thoughts and stop them. Start to practice being aware of the breath without making any change to slow it down or speed it up in any way. Just bring attention and awareness to the sensation of breathing without imposing any changes. This kind of relaxed awareness takes us deeper into the sensations and feelings of the body. Miraculously, this awareness is so powerful that when we are breathing there are absolutely no thoughts. Then as awareness on the breath increases, our breath rises and falls from the nostrils to the belly. A person who is anxious always breathes shallow from the chest alone. Breathing from the belly is a powerful healing for body, mind, and soul as the body, the brain, and the immune system is rejuvenated with more oxygen.

The Vedas say that when you breathe consciously, the breath that enters your body becomes the Prana – the vital life sustaining energy of the Creator.

Being aware and conscious of the breath brings us to the realization that we are absolutely being breathed, we do not need to do anything to breathe, we are being lived, and life lives through us every moment. It is humbling to notice that we are not the doers of anything and we are just a collection of patterns and memories. This liberates us from the thought that we are separate selves. It brings immense peace and freedom in the knowing that we are being breathed, moved, and lived every moment.

Breathing consciously we bring ourselves to the Present Moment – to the freedom from the unconsciousness of the ego.

Conscious breathing is a loving action, and it is a most powerful gift we can give ourselves!

With each conscious breath we choose life, we choose love, and we choose to liberate ourselves from the many burdens we carry. It is our birthright to be alive, to be loved, and to be in the Present Moment.

∞

RESPECTING THE EARTH

When all the trees have been cut down,
when all the animals have been hunted,
when all the waters are polluted,
when all the air is unsafe to breathe,
only then will you discover you cannot eat money.
~ Cree Prophecy

GAIA, is our Earth Mother. Every ancient mythology talks about the Earth Goddess who is the Great Mother of all creations. She gave birth to the sky, the sea, the land and all mortal creatures. All ancient sacred text and ancient religions around the world were based on Goddess worship which centered around the Earth.

The human body is made up of the Goddess' body which are the five elements; air, water, earth, fire, and space. The Earth is our Mother and respecting her and connecting with her helps us to become stronger.

For thousands of years we have lived in total disconnection with the Earth. Hence, we have destroyed, plundered, and tried to possess her, which in turn has wounded us.

Connecting with the heart of the Earth literally by visualizing a cord of light from our belly down to the heart of Gaia helps us to move beyond our fears and heal our wounds. This kind of visualization practiced everyday brings immense peace and it slows down the thought patterns that do not support us.

We can also connect with the Earth by taking the time to be with the stillness of nature. Connecting with nature brings immense healing to the body, mind, and soul.

In many Shamanic traditions, digging a hole on the ground and speaking or shouting our woes or illness into it and asking for help, is practiced as a very powerful method of healing.

Sitting down and placing both palms on the Earth and sending gratitude from the heart for a few minutes, will bring immense peace.

The Earth and everything around us is very much alive as the Earth is a very large being that is vibrant with life and wisdom of the Universe. We forgot to connect with the earth. We poke and plunder, mindlessly destroy forests, burn trees, apply fertilizer and pesticides, and we proceeded to make inventions to make things work. The earth is patient. It continues to absorb all of the negativity of human violence, war, and anger, but when it no longer has the strength to hold back, it erupts in volcanoes and earthquakes.

The earth is willing to co-create with us and is patiently waiting for us to wake up and align ourselves with our Divinity. Our loving attitudes give the earth the strength it needs. Since the Earth gave us her body, the more we communicate with her, the more we will link with our own powerful core, which is the God within.

Anastasia, the wisdom keeper of Russia, talks about our sacred connection to the Earth. Anastasia books by Vladimir Megre are a huge wake-up call to humanity. Many readers have completely rearranged their lives to reflect a more authentic connection to existence. Anastasia talks about the Dachniks. The Dachniks are people who consciously spend time with the Earth, touching the Earth with their hands with love, growing fruit and vegetable gardens to feed their family and neighbors all year long. They live in so much harmony that they do not use any mechanical contraptions. Anastasia relates that at one time in Russia, people were given tiny private plots that were too tiny to cultivate with mechanized equipments. The people were yearning for contact with the Earth and they took the tiny plots with great enthusiasm and millions of pairs of human (Dachnik) hands began touching the Earth with love. Lots and lots of people touched the Earth with their hands lovingly (not with mechanized tools), and the Earth felt it. She felt it very much, and the Earth felt new strength to carry on. Anastasia said that the Global catastrophe on the Earth was avoided in 1992 because of the Dachniks and the love they brought to the Earth.

The Earth may be big, but it is alive and very, very sensitive to love. It is also highly intelligent as it knows how to replenish itself and how to produce the right kind of food for the human body. The Earth also knows how to get rid of pests and weeds.

The entire Planet is created from the thought of God and it is created in perfection. When we align with our Divine Presence, we will be able to comprehend this and we will not spend much time and effort in searching for food, fertilizing the ground, or using pesticides. Our true purpose is to Co-create with existence.

The Tibetan Lamas' one special ritual everyday was to sit on the ground and touch the Earth with their palms spread wide and send loving thoughts to Mother Earth. The ancient peoples of the Planet lived in conscious connection with the Earth and they observed the cycles and rhythms of nature. They understood that the forests, meadows, fields, marshlands, and waterways were given to mankind not to be exploited for consumption, but to be taken care of harmoniously. Everything in existence on the Planet, the humans, rocks, trees, animals, minerals, herbs, and water, form a unified whole – only the mind stories separate them.

The Earth is now going through a Great Shift. Scientists and people in spiritual circles know that this is a huge shift – one that occurs once in 26,000 years. Usually in such a shift, the entire planet is wiped out of all life. But we have chosen to stay with the Earth and to consciously awaken ourselves. When we connect with the Earth everyday from our heart and mind, the Earth will carry us smoothly along with the shift, for the Earth is a Great wise being. The Planet is awakening into its Grand light of Oneness, and as a Divine being you were sent here to the Planet at the right time. Working our Divinity in physicality is what we came here to do. Forgetting our Divinity is the greatest illusion on this Planet. In the eyes of God, everyone is pure, holy, blameless, and childlike. Remember now that each of us are pure and holy. We help others to remember their Divinity only by seeing them with the eyes of God. May humanity remember! Let humanity awaken to its Divinity!

Gratitude ~ Iroquois Prayer

We return thanks to our mother, the earth,
which sustains us.
We return thanks to the rivers and streams,
which supply us with water.
We return thanks to all herbs,
which furnish medicines for the cure of our diseases.
We return thanks to the moon and stars,
which have given to us their light when the sun was gone.
We return thanks to the sun,
that has looked upon the earth with a beneficent eye.
Lastly, we return thanks to the Great Spirit, in Whom is embodied all goodness, and Who directs all things for the good of Her children.

∞

12 CELEBRATION

"Delight! Enjoy! God is not a thing. God is an attitude – an attitude of celebration and festivity. Drop all sadness. God is so close – dance! Drop long faces… It is sacrilege as He is so close by. Forget your childish miseries and worries; He is so close by. Don't go on brooding about immaterial things; He is so close by. Allow Him to hold your hand. He has been waiting for you for long." ~Osho

"If we couldn't laugh we would all go insane." ~Robert Frost

"I slept and I Dreamed that Life is All Joy. I Woke and I Saw that Life is All Service. I Served and I Saw That Service Is Joy." ~ Khalil Gibran

"The greatest prayer you could ever say would be to laugh every day. For when you do, it elevates the vibratory frequency within your being such that you could heal your entire body." ~Ramtha

∞

LOOKING AT THE MIRROR

The mirror is a most powerful medium that helps us to face our darkness within. It helps to see both the dark and the light sides that we are born with. It helps us to get acquainted with our multidimensional selves. The practice of looking at oneself through the mirror is a profound part of growth towards self-realization.

The fairy tale of *Snow White and the Seven Dwarfs* has in it a magic mirror – a reflective object that can answer any question. Truly, the mirror does answer all of our questions. It is good to look at oneself in the mirror when one is angry, when one is sad or distressed, and when one is happy. Take time to look at yourself in the mirror, and get to know and acknowledge every part and embrace all of the self with love and joy. Gazing at the mirror is a meditation in itself. It is considered to be a most profound psychic tool and has been used as such since ancient times. It brings enlightenment and spiritual awareness.

It takes courage to face the mirror and see all of ourselves as we truly are. When we come into the knowing of our Self, we can rejoice and celebrate the experience for it makes us stronger and wiser. Knowing our strengths and our weakness and accepting is true power. When we do not choose to know ourselves, we live in fear. We give away our power to people on the outside to tell us their version of who we are, and we live our lives according to the whims and fancies of others. This creates confusion and crisis in life.

This world is our mirror and there is no one out there; no one to please, and no one to prove to. Everything around us is a reflection of our image and even the one we consider our enemy, is actually our own reflection. Fairy tales are grand explanations of this. They show how the beast can be conquered by love, and they show the conquered beast to be one's own self. Everything we do is an act of self-definition. Our thoughts, emotions, and words carry the energy of creation. Each moment of life is sacred and new. It carries amazing potentials and we are born to life every moment. The illusions of the mirror are our tools, and they were meant to help us evolve into our grander selves. The ultimate truth is that there is no separation; there is only Unity and Oneness with all things and with the Creator.

Meditation

The following meditations help one to realize the All is One.

1. Practice gazing at yourself in the mirror. Gaze at yourself in the mirror and imagine yourself to become the person in the mirror. Perceive yourself in the mirror looking at the real you outside the mirror. Shift your attention back into your body. Do this as many times as you can. This meditation helps us with our ability to connect with the watcher within.

2. Every night before going to sleep, close your eyes and look at your day backwards like a tape rewinding. When you come upon a difficult situation with someone, stand in that person's place. Look at yourself from that person's vantage point. You can now see yourself clearly as the person sees you. The person is your mirror.

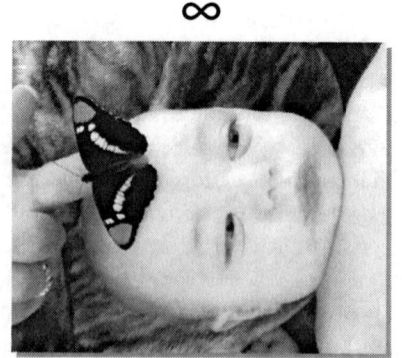

∞

MAGICAL KINGDOM AND FAIRY TALES

Fairy tales are about imagination, dreams, magic, and creativity. Children all over the world love them, they love to read them, and they love to hear them again and again. There is nothing impossible in a fairy tale as it goes beyond the mundane world and brings immense joy to children's hearts. Children come fresh from the spirit world and their memories are still fresh with their angel friends, magic, and fairies. Children expect magic and believe in miracles. Many children see angels, fairies, and other beings of the formless dimensions. They converse and play with them, but as they grow up, the adults who have lost touch with magic do not see these things so they dissuade the children from talking about magic. As we grew up, due to social conditioning, we stopped believing in magic. We stopped believing in the formless, and learned to trust only the physical senses. We need to remember that physicality is only a miniscule part of who we are. And we need to remember that our greater being lives in the formless dimensions.

Transforming one possibility into another is the alchemical magic that we forgot as we grew older. Magic is not some fantasy – it is very real. The entire universe is magical, and we tap into the magic of the universe by getting our beliefs and mind stories out of the way. By emptying ourselves of mind stories and totally inviting the eternal goodness of the universe, we create magic and miracles in our life. Hence, magic is not a fantasy but it is the gift that life is waiting to give us. When we realize this and remove our mind stories of how things should or should not be, we enter into the Magical Kingdom of Life. This is the Kingdom Consciousness taught by all of the great masters of the world. Living from Kingdom Consciousness like a little child with complete trust and excitement, makes every need fulfilled, every wish satisfied, and every dream realized. Living from Kingdom Consciousness brings enough and more of eternal goodness into our life. By first accepting and then understanding that all things are possible, we are then able to intentionally transform one possibility into another. By learning to simply change one thought, feeling, or belief into another, we begin to understand how to effortlessly create and sustain Well-Being, Abundance, and Joy. When we know our truth, the truth will bring us freedom. Our truth is the grandest illumination for our life.

∞

Kit Alderson
THE ANSWER TO WORLD CRISIS

Inner peace begins the moment you choose to not allow situations in life or another person's opinion to control your emotions. Choosing not to engage with the emotions of the collective, also not to engage in your own emotions, and allowing emotions to dissipate is the best way to peace. Hanging on to someone else's truth as we perceive it, will not help us in any way. The external world is no longer our truth. Old ways do not work, and whatever is in the external world is the past. It is an old dream of someone else's. We are born with gifts to dream grander visions and create greater versions of ourselves.

We arrive into this physical Planet with nothing, and we leave with nothing. During the time of living on the planet, we are constantly pressured to achieve and claim many things. Society stresses us to possess, dominate, and have more than others have. It may be money or it may be virtue, yet it does not matter.

Our education system is rooted in the idea of competition. The idea to compete, possess, achieve, accomplish, compare, and claim creates immense misery. So even though you achieve, possess, accomplish, and claim, you continue to be miserable and your anxiety becomes a habit. Even though you may have achieved a great education, a high paying job, or a million dollar home, you remain cautious, anxious, and afraid. The quality of your outer world may have changed, but the quality of your inner world is in lack.

When we are out of alignment with the Divine Presence, which is our true self, our belief systems take over and we live in the energy of fear. Fear is our indicator – fear indicates to us that we are holding on to something that is not in alignment with our true self.

We are made of the material of the Universe, and the universe is made of eternal goodness. It is not possible for us to be not okay. Thinking "I am not okay" is a learned thought that came from someone else, and we believed them. The stories of the mind are created for us to fit in with the world outside. There is no expansion here as it is the same old story of fear and pain that stagnates our journey.

Time is a container for our beliefs. Beliefs held in time are now collapsing because of the planetary changes. The old beliefs are dissolving and something new and far more beautiful is coming our way. Let go of old beliefs and realize that when we are not in the place of our power, we attach to random and unfocused thoughts that bring fear. The spiritual tools that are shared in this book are a great help in these changing times. Choosing to live from the place of eternal goodness can happen only in the Present moment. Being in the center of the head is a powerful tool that helps us to be in the Present or the Now. Connecting with the heart helps to keep us calm and connected to our Higher Self. Practicing to be aware of our breath keeps us in the Present moment and connected to the Creator's healing love and light.

Taking time to discover your true nature awakens you to remembering that there is nobody doing anything to you. You speak your fears aloud and ask how they serve your life at this time and in understanding them, you discover the effortlessness of life. When you give away your power to people outside you, your power is used to scare you. The body is only a temporary costume; therefore, it is wise to connect with the True Self who knows and trusts that life is full of eternal goodness. The True Self knows that real intelligence is effortless.

This Great Planetary Shift requires our attention. All of the programs of the old world are being removed and massive creative energies of eternal goodness are being poured into the Planet. It is very important how we hold our attention point during this transition as our focus is a magnifier.

There is no scarcity, lack of abundance, or lack of opportunity on the Planet. Remove definitions on how things should happen or can happen, and stretch your definitions to creatively imagine and include unexpected ways, magical ways, and miraculous ways that act on joy.

There is no gloom and doom crisis at a global level. It is simply time to activate our new creative potentials.

Creation is absolutely tuned to our wishes as nothing we love can be taken away from us. You do not need to get rid of things; you only need to transform them. Nothing is ever born and nothing dies. Everything is held in existence lovingly for you to play with – everything is there, absolutely everything. You play with existence by giving it your meaning and by remembering that you have the ability to transform and create.

The sooner we understand this, the sooner we embrace what is true. Turn your attention to what you love and it will start producing for you. Expand to what is possible instead of limiting your point of view to beliefs about how things must be done.

Represent joy, celebration, and excitement in all that you do. Existence is excitement. Your beliefs create your reality and when you allow for unexpected things to happen, you create magic.

Abundance is the ability to do what you need to do and to do it when you need to. If you think you do not have the things to do what you need to do, then you create limitedness. Get out of limitedness by choosing to allow joy and to allow excitement by bringing your focus to the present moment. And be in the place of excited anticipation.

Find your joy, do the best you do, enjoy yourself, and help others to enjoy. Before you know it, you will be making a living doing what you do well, and you will be completely supported. However, if you carry a belief system which states that what you are doing does not count, then you are limiting your abundance.

Just act on the excitement, simply allow the excitement, and it will bring to you all that you need. Excited anticipation will bring to you your support and your abundance.

∞

Dawn Haliburton-Rudy
CELEBRATION AND JOY

Joy represents God as the Creator created us in Joy. When you live in joy, you live in the Presence of God. Follow your highest joy to find the Magical Kingdom of the Creator within. Joy is a state of Mind. The Prime Creator, Sadashiva, is ever joy. In Sanskrit, Sadasiva means: sada – ever; siva – joy. As Sadashiva created us in joy, we are joy. Joy is another name of the Creator.

We need nothing to be in joy as we are joy itself. When we realize that joy is not created as a result of certain conditions, we understand that when we choose to live from the state of Joy, joyous conditions are created around us! The secret to create joyous conditions around us is to choose to be in the state of joy as the creator made us.

The True Self has no need of any love or appreciation from the outside. There is a huge wellspring of love and joy within the Self that can embrace this whole Universe.

We are the ones we are seeking. The only true love affair is the one with the Self and not with anything on the outside. Without the busyness of the mind, we all are pure love.

At every given moment choose joy, choose excitement, and choose peace. The next moment is created only from this moment. This present moment is important. Excitement and joy is the energy that leads you to your True Self. Excitement and joy leads you to the Creator regardless of whatever the issue is and regardless of the situation's outward appearance.

At one time I had a neighbor who had a little dog who was so happy to see every one she met. She would wag her tail, jump up and down, and look at you with such loving, knowing eyes. The little dog was so excited with life and she was so much in gratitude for everything around her that everyone fell in love with this little dog. This little dog had brought in such a powerful reminder of joy into my life. I found that anytime I felt uncomfortable or sad with my mind stories, I could immediately switch my thoughts to the exuberant joy of this little dog. In my mind's eye, I saw her wag her little tail and excitedly jump up and down, and as she was so happy with life and showed it with her entire body, it brought me joy, excitement, and trust in the eternal goodness of Divine Love. I chose to give gratitude to life like this little dog. Immediately, my mood changed and I became so happy and thankful toward life. I am so much in gratitude to this little being that showed me to live in excitement for life.

Excitement lets you know that the one here, now, in this Present Time, is the true you. By choosing joy, you are acknowledging your true self to the Universe. It is then that the Universe has the conviction that it is you, and it is then that the Universe can support who you actually are rather than supporting who you have been told you have to be. Events come and go, but consciousness is what binds and creates all events. It is important to hold the right consciousness that leads you to your joy and to your abundance. The secret key to enter your Magic Kingdom is imagination and trust to create joy in all events of life.

This planet's playground has no built-in meaning. It takes the meaning you choose to give it, and this is the highest form of love and dignity. You experience your body's natural life force energy by the sensation called excitement when you are in harmony and balance with yourself. However, you experience the energy as stress and anxiety when you attach your emotions to the belief systems and others' opinions about you. It is when you are out of tune with your natural self that fear comes and shows you that you are out of alignment with your Divine Presence. Know that you have freewill, and know that you create your reality all of the time. When you find yourself stuck or blocked, it is because of the meaning you have given to the situation. You are out of alignment with your Divine Presence. Find out what you can do to relate to the situation in a more joyful way to achieve alignment.

> "You have sole ownership of your vision. And the Universe will give you what you want within your vision. What happens with most people is that they muddy their vision with "reality." Their vision becomes full of not only what they want but what everybody else thinks about what they

want, too. Your work is to clarify and purify your vision so that the vibration that you are offering can then be answered. Change does not come from the reality; change comes from within you. When you choose to do the things of change regardless of how the reality may seem to look, your reality will reflect your change." ~Abraham-Hicks

Identify your purpose and become aware of your current situation. Take account of things that do not support you and take account of things that uplift you. Then choose to do more of the things that uplift you. Do not wait for the world to uplift you, you have the power to transform your life.

∞

Diana Beardsley

SMILE - A SPIRITUAL TOOL TO TRANSFORM STRESS

"Don't wait for the reflection in the mirror to smile first, smile first regardless of there being any mirrors or not"
~Bashar

"A smile from the soul is spiritual relaxation." ~The Siddha

The Siddha suggests that we learn to smile in the sweet way of a child to make everything bright and beautiful around us.

Every time we smile at someone, we are bringing a beautiful gift of peace to that person. It brings sunshine into their lives.

A smile is the most inexpensive and most attractive cosmetic you can wear all day. It is the most beautiful jewel on the face, and it makes you the most attractive person in the world. Smiling is a special language of humans. The more this language is practiced, the more love, joy, peace, happiness, and harmony are anchored on the Planet. Smile for no reason, keep smiling even when people are not around, and you will be surprised. Energetically, smiling attracts wisdom and joy into your life. A smile is a very powerful spiritual tool. It anchors the timeless Presence of the higher dimensions. In our busy mechanical lives we forget this tool.

Have you ever noticed that when seeing a picture where people are smiling, it automatically makes us smile and brings happiness to that moment?

Any time when you feel that the energy around you is dense, you will notice that the moment you squeezed in a smile, the entire atmosphere within you and around you became lighter and full of ease. Simply bring a smile to your face during any moment of stress, confusion, or an argument. Just do it and you will see the magic. You can post a smiley face, write the word *SMILE*, or any other method of reminder near your bed, your work place, or on your fridge to remind you to smile and keep yourself in a place of ease and grace. Choose to smile for no reason – just smile. Smiling is a powerful gift that you can give yourself today. It is a tool for the instant transformation of stress.

Let us choose to practice this powerful and ancient Spiritual tool of smiling everyday at all times to bless our Planet and us!

∞

LAUGHTER MEDITATION

LAUGHTER is a powerful tool. It has been given as a gift only to humans. No one has heard plants or animals laugh at any time. When we laugh we come back to our true self. Laughter is infectious and when someone sees you laugh they are also motivated to laugh, and when they laugh their stress level is reduced, and you have given them a gift of well-being in their life.

Laughter provides great physical and emotional release. Laughter is a higher state of consciousness and when one is able to hold that state of consciousness, the person becomes lighter, and can vibrate in a place of absolute well being.

The mind stories disappear when there is laughter. Life becomes magical and full of fun when we choose to hold the vibration of laughter. Laughter takes us to a state of egoless innocence and to a non-judgmental attitude. When we laugh, we become like little children as suddenly the mind disappears. In reality, laughter brings solutions to all kinds of physical, mental, emotional, and spiritual problems.

Medical research has revealed that laughter reduces the level of stress hormones and increases the level of health enhancing hormones like endorphins and neurotransmitters. Laughter also increases the number of antibody producing cells which promotes a strong immune system thereby bringing amazing healing and well-being in the physical body.

A good belly laugh works our abs, shoulders, and makes our muscles more relaxed. It is a good work out for the heart muscles also.

Many people try to do meditation and have failed because it sounds to be very serious, but when laughter is tried as a meditation, there will be complete benefit for body, mind and soul. Practicing laughter for no reason is a powerful meditation. Great teachers like the Zen Master Hotei, who is called as the Laughing Buddha, taught the simple technique of enlightenment through laughter. According to Hotei, "laughter is our birthright" and no matter what happens in our life, we must come back to laughter. In many Zen monasteries the monks begin their day with laughter and end their day with laughter.

By choosing laughter, we bring Heaven into our lives and into this Planet.

Laughing at somebody is not good, laughing for a reason is intellectual and from the mind, but laughing without a reason is spiritual.

The Indian mystic Bagwan Shree Rajneesh also called as OSHO, devised a meditation out of laughter. It is very easy and delightful to do. It is a very powerful meditation!

Meditation

Laugh for no reason at all. Go in and find your own laughter inside. Allow the laughter to bubble up from the inside. Create a giggle in the very guts of your being, as if your whole body is giggling, laughing. Start swaying with that laughter; let it spread from the belly to the whole of your body. Go crazily into it. For thirty minutes do the laughing. If it comes uproariously, loudly, allow it. If it comes silently, then sometimes silently, simply laugh for thirty minutes every day. See your life transform into joy and excitement.

∞

SIMPLE REMINDERS TO MANIFEST YOUR MIRACLES EVERYDAY

1. Take a few moments to dwell upon feelings of appreciation and gratitude throughout your day.
2. Take time to place your awareness on your breathing – practice Pranic breathing for at least 5 minutes.
3. Place your hands on your heart – take a moment to listen to your heart beat and smile at your heart.
4. Create a space for you to sit in silence and center yourself – practice seeing the world from the center of your head.
5. Practice gazing at yourself in the mirror – every time you look into your eyes say, "I love You."

∞

A MANIFESTING TOOL

Based on the fundamental understanding that the mirror of the universe reflects your consciousness, there exists many simple ways to manifest your desires by using the mirror as your tool. We wish to share one such simple and most effective tool here:

Practice gazing at yourself in the mirror and imagine yourself to become the person in the mirror. Perceive yourself in the mirror looking at the real you outside of the mirror. Shift your attention back into your body. Do this as many times as you can.

Ground yourself and breathe consciously for a few minutes, place your hands on your heart, connect with your heart, and smile at your heart. Be in the place of Gratitude knowing that you are a beloved child of the Universe, that you are a limitless being, and that infinite possibilities are available for you. See the Universe enveloping you in a huge sphere that surrounds you.

Now, see the mirror as a huge crystal ball in front of you. Place a mirror image of yourself inside this crystal ball and imagine yourself living your chosen reality. See yourself having the object, the situation, or the ability you desire with you at this time (it is important to note here that the object cannot be persons you know of as this technique cannot be used to control the behavior of others or to cause them to do something against their will). The intention of this tool is for self-realization and manifesting the most positive aspect of the self.

Energize this image inside the crystal ball with pure intention and breathe the Pranic breath and allow the love and light from your heart center to flow to this crystal ball. In this moment the cosmic energies of the Universe align with your heart center, they answer your call/desire. By the very nature of holding your consciousness in your heart center, infinite possibilities are available for you. Hold the image for as long as you can, then let go.

Continue to work with this tool each day. The image in the crystal ball becomes a powerful magnet that attracts benevolent universal energies by bringing in unexpected situations, persons, and opportunities for manifesting your desired reality.

Be careful of what you ask for as you will receive it!

∞

THE COSMIC COMEDY OF LIFE

Time, dimension, physicality, and everything is an illusion and it is a reflection of our consciousness. It is time for us to wake up from our fascination with drama, conflict, and pain. This reality is our playground, we are the creators here, only we are real, we are pure love, and we are never separate from God-Creator. There is only Oneness with God, and we all are a part of the one body of the Creator. So everything that happens in the one body is a decision of the all. Every experience that we call as happiness, love, peace, and harmony is actually a decision and not an experience. There is nothing outside of the one body to call for a reaction and the only decision made is to be in joy, to be in happiness, and to be in peace. The ultimate truth is that the one is the all and the all is the one. We are beings of unlimited possibilities and when we allow our possibilities to expand, the world will mirror it to us. It is thus clear that we never do anything for anyone; therefore, whatever we do for another is actually what we do for ourselves. And when we choose to surrender, we are actually accepting our total self and not abandoning or giving up ourselves. Being in our true self is following our joy, our love, our excitement, and our bliss as this is our very nature. When we choose to live from our true selves, our joy, love, excitement, and bliss is multiplied in abundance and the mirror outside has to absolutely support this decision. When we realize that we are in oneness with everything and that there is nothing outside us that is not us, then our self-interest changes. So instead of competing with others to get what we want, we give what we want to others. Instead of seeking success or power for ourselves, we seek to empower others and make them successful. Instead of searching for love, comfort, peace, or satisfaction, we become the givers of these things to others. And because of the ultimate truth that all is the one and one is the all, what we give out we receive back multiplied. We wake up to this truth, and we understand that we are the ones we were waiting for. This understanding is the cosmic comedy of life.

We realize that our limitations are self-imposed, that there is absolutely no one to rescue, nothing to achieve, nowhere to be, that all learning is truly only a remembering, and that we are unlimited and infinite beings with our awakening in our own hands. Realizing this we can laugh the biggest laugh at ourselves and at life as this is the comedy that was hidden from us. Aligning with our Divine Presence, we understand and learn to laugh at life. This is the key to enlightenment.

Life is a grand celebration. This moment is precious and powerful, it designs the next moment. Our only true purpose is to celebrate life, to bring in love, joy, and laughter into every aspect of life so that the dark sky of unconsciousness may break into the brilliant light of understanding. Joy and laughter are of the highest vibration of existence. Anchoring joy and laughter is the grandest prayer and it represents trust and devotion to the Divine. When we smile or laugh, our mind stops its stories, we anchor the light of the higher dimensions, and we invite inner peace. We need not seek for paradise for we are born with the gifts to create paradise here now.

May we choose to fill our moments with love, joy, and laughter! May well-being and inner peace be our companions! May the blessings Be!

~With Acknowledgement and Gratitude to~

A Course In Miracles ~ Foundation for Inner Peace -acim.org/
Seth
Abraham
Carl Jung
Joseph Campbell
Khalil Gibran
Mahatma Gandhi
John Lennon
Rumi ~ Mevlana Jalal-e-Din Mevlavi
The Pleiadians via Christine Day
Eckhart Tolle -www.eckharttolle.com/
His Holiness the Dalai Lama -www.dalailama.com/
Osho -www.osho.com/
Louise Hay -www.louisehay.com/
Jim Self -www.masteringalchemy.com/
Gregg Braden -www.greggbraden.com/
Shakti Gawain -www.shaktigawain.com/
Marianne Williamson -www.marianne.com/
Dr. Mitchell Gibson -www.tybro.com
Deepak Chopra, M.D., F.A.C.P. -www.deepakchopra.com/
Jill Bolte Taylor -drjilltaylor.com/
Byron Katie -www.thework.com
Dr. Joseph Murphy -josephmurphy.wwwhubs.com/
Catherine Shainberg -www.schoolofimages.com/bio.html
Thich Nhat Hanh -www.mindfulnessbell.org/thay.php
Falun Dafa -en.falundafa.org/falun-dafa-video-audio.html
Drunvalo Melchizedek -www.drunvalo.net/
Master Mooji -www.stillnessspeaks.com/mooji/
Quantum K Healing -www.quantumk.co.uk/quantumk_video.htm
Dr. Ihaleakala Hew Len -www.hooponoponoway.net
Dr. Cleve Backster -www.livepsyche.com/blog/spirituality/beyond-the-five-senses/biocommunication-ability-2/
Dr. Paul Pearsall -www.paulpearsall.com/

ABOUT THE AUTHORS

At a very early age, Premlatha Rajkumar understood that she had come for a very specific purpose; to connect with her Divinity here in the physical world and thereby help awaken others around her. Her thirst for a closer connection with the heart of the Creator lead her into the Presence of many masters and teachers of spiritual disciplines. Right from her younger days, she had noticed that she remembered her travels in the astral planes during her dreamtime. She also had the opportunity to meet many masters and teachers in the astral and bring back the memories for her work here on the Planet at this time. In her dreamtime travels, she had the grand opportunity to communicate and be in the Presence of many benevolent celestial beings and ascended masters like Yeshua, Lord Sananda, Chief White Eagle, Lady Portia, Master Seraphis Bey, the Medicine Buddha, Paramhansa Yogananda, Lord Krishna, Lord Ganesha, The Three Maggis of the East, Goddess Durga, Goddess Andal, Bhagwan Shree Rajneesh, Goddess Quan Yin, and many Bodhisattvas. She uses the tools given to her by these beloved beings to help humanity's awakening at this time.

The Author, Premlatha Rajkumar, was born in 1965 in Coimbatore, a City in the State of Tamil Nadu, India. She has a Masters Degree in Child Development and Family Relationships and has a teaching degree. She taught college and school students for more than fifteen years in India, and at that time, many benefited from her counsel on life lessons. In 2002, she moved to the USA with her family. She is known among friends as an Energy Healer, Energy Teacher and Spiritual Life Coach. For more than thirty years, she has given many thousands of Energy healings and has counseled thousands as a Spiritual Life coach. With her intuitive gifts, she reaches out to others and teaches Energy work and meditation. At present, she lives in Texas with her husband

and two children.

Over many years of studying a multitude of spiritual disciplines such as Reiki, Magnified Healing, Pranic Healing, practicing twin heart meditation, working with crystals, practicing Sahaja Yoga of mother Nirmala Devi, connecting and communicating with Angelic beings, elemental beings, working with the Medicine Buddha, working with the power of the Miracle Prayer, practicing Qi Gong, practicing Falun Dafa, practicing Alchemy, and by what she has learned from her own life journey, Premlatha helps bring people to a closer connection with the Creator-God. As a Spiritual life coach, she helps people to heal and bring balance into their lives by bringing body, mind and spirit together. One of her spiritual workings on this Planet is to assist departing souls to heal, and to assist new souls to enter the Planet.

From 2009 – 2011 she has worked on Mastering Alchemy Level 1 and Level 2 with Jim Self, the founder of Mastering Alchemy. Alchemy is a way of life to step from a third dimensional experience into a higher more expansive awareness of life. Practicing alchemy accelerates our ascension as multidimensional beings from this third dimensional human game of duality. At present, she is dedicated in aiding humanity and the Planet in establishing harmony, peace, and prosperity through her work with the Archangels and her energy work with alchemy and sacred geometry. She provides energy healing, counseling, and guidance for people who come to her personally or connect with her on the Internet. She is also involved in practicing and sharing her wisdom and her knowledge about simple but powerful spiritual tools that can support and accelerate spiritual evolution at this time on the Planet. Premlatha is also a member of the Organ of Spiritual Protection of the Council of Imhotep and Maat founded by Dr. Mitchell Gibson.

A spiritual shift is occurring on the Planet. People around the world are experiencing expansiveness within themselves. The solutions of the past are not working anymore, it is an entirely new world being created out there, and it is moving everyone to stand in their truth. The old energy of playing the game of "I do not know who I am" is being dissolved. There is a greater need now for humanity to align with Spirit and with their Higher Selves, to know the truth of who they are, and to know their connection with the Creator, other humans, all other created beings, and experiencing oneness with the Planet. We are entering into the Golden Age of Spiritual Alignment and awakening to our True Selves.

Premlatha considers this book as guidance from her Celestial Soul to bless the awakening humanity at this time with the techniques and knowledge given to her to help people remember their true purpose. For the co-creation of this book, her Celestial Soul brought in the Presence of the wise and beautiful Sheryl Lynn Christian, the co-author of this book.

∞

Essentially a teacher, author Sheryl Lynn Christian's strengths are compassion, clarity, openness, and creativity. Coming from a place of kindness and love, she listens, empathizes, and understands the issue, and she uses her intuitive skills to creatively seek and help people find their solution. This practice builds trust and mutual respect, has served many, and will remain her approach. She is currently pursuing her Ph.D. in Psychology with a research emphasis on the cognitive processes of creative expression.

Since 1989, Sheryl Lynn Christian continues to be a lifetime scholar and "miracle worker" of A Course In Miracles (ACIM) – a psycho-spiritual guide to inner peace. For twenty-three years, she has felt that her Divinely True Purpose is to heal the world. Opening to her higher self, the inner voice, and the angelic guides who are and have been with her always, she began her journey long ago by placing her trust in God, and she asked to be led where she needed to go. By doing all things with loving intent and starting with some of the same self-love practice techniques described in this book, she achieved a true sense of wholeness and peace.

In the early 1990s, she became a Certified Practitioner of Neuro Linguistic Programming Therapy® and a facilitator of Time Line Therapy™ and studied Western Astrology at Tenth House Consulting with Diane Ronngren. She is a Past Life Coach and Medium certified by clairvoyant, numerologist, Eastern Astrologer, and Ayurvedic healer,

Prince Raja Harindra Singh, Ph.D. As an intuitive and vibrational healer, Sheryl has worked with spiritual Astrologist and vibrational healer, Eduardo J. Caldera, and she is an instructor of Western Astrology and Tarot.

As spirit guided her, for over fifteen years Sheryl worked in the human services field in several capacities; as a volunteer and a trainer for the C.A.S.A. program, as a Certified Mental Health Crisis Para-Professional, and for twelve years she was a Caseworker in Child Welfare. As a Child Protection Caseworker, she spent the last five years as a certified Court Ordered supervised visitation specialist. She is regarded as a Court expert witness in the areas of child welfare and protection, supervised visitation, and on the effects of domestic violence and sexual abuse on children. She is also a certified instructor for Art Innovators – an art enrichment program for children and adults.

Sheryl Lynn Christian was raised in Los Angeles. She is the mother of four beautiful and loving children who are now grown. Most of her psycho-spiritual training was attended in Los Angeles. She and her children moved from California to rural Arkansas in 1992. In Arkansas, she met "Prince" Harindra Singh, Ph.D. and studied under him. "Prince" directed her to become an author and to adopt a pen name to write under. As an author and an artist, she has published four books thus far under her pen name, primarily romantic historical fiction, and she illustrates the covers as well as creates images of her characters. Most of her ideas have come from her past-life experiences, dreams, fantasies, and visions. She is a mentor for Classic Insights, a spiritual college with an emphasis on the arts, and she is also a member of the Spiritual Emergencies Group - Council of Imhotep and Ma'at founded by Dr. Mitchell Gibson.

From the place of peace, deservedness, and gratitude, the concept and title of *Twelve Steps to Inner Peace* came to Sheryl as a gentle whisper, and she was guided to ask Premlatha Rajkumar to join her in writing this important and potentially world healing book. When asked, Premlatha excitedly said that she had already begun writing and that she'd outlined *twelve* chapters! And she said that she was waiting for someone to assist her in putting it together!

In a sacred, miraculous, and divine fashion, the book, *Twelve Steps to Inner Peace*, was co-created… And so it is…